Memoria Futuri
CATHOLIC-JEWISH DIALOGUE
YESTERDAY, TODAY, AND TOMORROW

Studies in
Judaism and Christianity

*Exploration of Issues in the
Contemporary Dialogue Between
Christians and Jews*

Editors
Kevin A. Lynch, CSP
Michael McGarry, CSP
Mark-David Janus, CSP
Yehezkel Landau
Dr. Peter Pettit
Dr. Elena Procario-Foley
Dr. Ann Riggs

A STIMULUS BOOK

Memoria Futuri
CATHOLIC-JEWISH DIALOGUE YESTERDAY, TODAY, AND TOMORROW

Texts and Addresses of Cardinal William H. Keeler

Selected and edited by Eugene J. Fisher

A Stimulus Book

Paulist Press ◆ New York ◆ Mahwah, NJ

Cover design by Sharyn Banks
Cover photograph courtesy of Hebrew Union College-Jewish Institute of Religion. Used with permission.

Library of Congress Cataloging-in-Publication Data

Keeler, William H. (William Henry), 1931–
    Memoria futuri : Catholic-Jewish dialogue yesterday, today, and tomorrow : texts and addresses of Cardinal William H. Keeler / selected and edited by Eugene J. Fisher.
        p. cm.
    "A Stimulus book."
    ISBN 978-0-8091-4769-4 (alk. paper)
    1. Catholic Church—Relations—Judaism. 2. Judaism—Relations—Catholic Church. 3. Christianity and antisemitism. I. Fisher, Eugene J. II. Title.
    BM535.K38 2012
    261.2`6—dc23

                                                                    2012004037

Published by Paulist Press
997 Macarthur Boulevard
Mahwah, New Jersey 07430

www.paulistpress.com

Printed and bound in the
United States of America

Contents

Foreword

This volume spans the years from 1987 to 2005, when Cardinal William H. Keeler was episcopal moderator for Catholic-Jewish Relations for the U.S. Conference of Catholic Bishops, during which he was also its president for three years. I have selected these texts and edited them to fit a volume of this size. Three major essays are not included, since they have been published in other books and are therefore widely available: "Catholic-Jewish Relations in the Twentieth Century," in Aron Hirt-Manheimer, ed., *Essays on Contemporary Judaism Honoring Rabbi Alexander M. Schindler* (New York: UAHC Press, 1995); "Dialogue," in Anthony J. Cernera, ed., *Toward Greater Understanding: Essays in Honor of John Cardinal O'Connor* (Fairfield, CT: Sacred Heart University Press, 1995); and "New Moments in Catholic-Jewish Relations," in Zvia Ginor, ed., *Yakar Le'Mordecai: Jubilee Volume in Honor of Rabbi Mordecai Waxman, Essays on Jewish thought, American Judaism and Jewish-Christian Relations* (New York: KTAV, 1998).

The title of this volume, *Memoria Futuri*, means "remembering the past for the sake of the future." It is both a leitmotif in Cardinal Keeler's work and an apt description of the nature of the Catholic-Jewish dialogue that he steered for the American bishops and thus, to a real extent, for the Catholic Church as a whole in its most crucial time of expansion and transformation—the period during the pontificate of Pope John Paul II. As a young priest from Harrisburg, Pennsylvania, Father Keeler was a *peritus* (theological expert) at the Second Vatican Council, and the vision and spirit of the Council has defined and shaped his life, especially with regard to Catholic-Jewish relations.

The Catholic Church has produced many theologians, bishops, and cardinals over the centuries. Few have had such an impact on such a core aspect of the life of the Church as Cardinal Keeler has had. The texts and addresses in this volume will, I believe, give some indication of how and why he had such an impact on the Catholic world, nationally and internationally.

As the staff person for the bishops' conference during the years when Cardinal Keeler was episcopal moderator, I can attest to his great gifts—not only his dialoguing with Jews, since he has been open to understanding and to the deeper feelings beneath intellectual understanding, but also, equally importantly, to his being able to communicate to the Holy See what was really on the minds of Jews and in their hearts, and the reasons for their concerns. With such understanding the Holy See was able, as often as not, to respond adequately, and sometimes even more than adequately, to the situations and crises and opportunities of its newly established relationship with the people out of whom Christianity arose.

Eugene Fisher
Saint Leo University, June 14, 2011

1
Mobilization for Soviet Jewry

On behalf of the National Conference of Catholic Bishops, I am privileged to speak in support of your concern for the basic human rights of those who, half a world away, are your brothers and sisters—and mine. Whether we speak for Jew or Baptist or Catholic, or for any others who suffer because of their faith or ethnic origin, whether they be in Moscow or Leningrad or Vilnius or Kiev or in a thousand other places, our hearts must ache, our voices must rise, because they are our brothers and sisters, and because they suffer.

Long ago the Psalmist exulted in the enormous dignity that is each individual's:

> For it was you who formed my inward parts;
>   you knit me together in my mother's womb.
> I praise you, for I am fearfully and wonderfully made.
> Wonderful are your works.   (Ps 139:13–14)

That wondrous dignity, of God's own making, we lift up today. We remember also God's providence in the liberating Exodus of his people long ago and pray that it may be renewed in our day.

Our common witness now reflects a vision shared in Miami in September by Rabbi Mordecai Waxman and Pope John Paul II—a vision that the pope summed up as this:

We are called to collaborate in service and to unite in a common cause wherever a brother or sister is unattended, forgotten, neglected or suffering in any way; wherever human rights are endangered or human dignity offended; wherever the rights of God are violated or ignored.[1]

That is why we are here today! That is why we show our solidarity with Soviet Jewry and with all others in that land whose freedom is impaired.

With the Psalmist I now repeat:

Let me hear what God the LORD will speak,
    for he will speak peace to his people,
    to his faithful, to those who turn to him in their hearts.

(Ps 85:8)

Shalom!

Washington, DC, December 6, 1987

2
An Address to the Anti-Defamation League

National Executive Committee

I am grateful for the invitation to be with you today. On a number of occasions—in Rome, at Castel Gandolfo, and in reporting to the body of the bishops of the United States—I have had an opportunity to affirm the helpful role of the Anti-Defamation League (ADL) in many different ways. The exchange of letters between Archbishop May and Pope John Paul II last summer, which occurred at the time of the publication of the pope's book *On Jews and Judaism*,[1] reminded many of the leadership of the ADL of the positive steps taken by the Catholic Church in fulfillment of the commitments made at the Second Vatican Council.

It is as a pastor that I come to this discussion today. Part of my personal pilgrimage through life has been an unfolding of an understanding of the issues that are part of our discussion today. As a young priest, I visited the tomb of Father Rupert Mayer, SJ (1876–1945), who preached against the Nazis and was imprisoned at Dachau, and whose tomb in Munich is today a place of pilgrimage. He was beatified by Pope John Paul II earlier this year. In 1961, a priest friend and I visited the home of Anne Frank in Amsterdam, standing in silence to pray that what happened to her, taken away in the innocence of youth to the gas chambers of Auschwitz, would never happen again.

I was a *peritus* at the Second Vatican Council. At the outset of the Council in 1962, at the request of Pope John XXIII, Cardinal Augustin Bea introduced the theme of relations between the Catholic Church and the Jewish people. This began the history of *Nostra Aetate*, the Declaration on the Relation of the Church to Non-Christian Religions,[2] which was passed only at the end of the Council in October of 1965, but which would chart a new course for internal renewal within the Church and for our relations with Jews. Coming back from the Council, we began formal Catholic-Jewish efforts in Harrisburg, Pennsylvania, so that in 1967, during the Six Days' War, I participated in a rally of the Jewish community and heard memories of the Holocaust and the fear of its repetition. Over the years I have given hundreds of talks to Catholic and other audiences on the Second Vatican Council, always with an explanation of the basic points of *Nostra Aetate*.

The understandably strong Jewish reaction to the 1987 meeting between Pope John Paul II and President Kurt Waldheim, whose Nazi past came out just at the time of the meeting, offered an opportunity for us to explain to Catholics the feelings of Jewish people regarding the Holocaust.[3] In trying to interpret the Holocaust for Catholics, I have found that the analogy of *sacrament* is most helpful. I tell my listeners that Jews regard as a sacrilege anything that seems to tarnish or diminish the memory of the Holocaust. Waldheim became for many a symbol of trying to sweep memories of the Holocaust under the carpet.

To Jews, it is necessary to explain the feelings of Catholics. The pope has an office with great spiritual significance to our people. We Catholics see the role of the pope, whom we call with meaning our Holy Father, in the context of our faith and devotional life. Many times during the discussions of June and July in 1987, some of our Jewish partners in dialogue tried to reassure us that they had good relationships with American Catholics but not with the pope. As I tried to explain the feelings that this kind of remark automatically triggered in a Catholic, one rabbi said, "I think I understand. Many of our people feel that when one attacks the State of Israel, that person is also attacking basic Jewish identity."

So I invite the Jewish members of this audience to see our Holy Father as we Catholics see and know him. He is the one who, from a hospital bed, forgave the man who shot him. He is one who, like his predecessors, has met and shaken hands with heads of state who were actively persecuting Catholics. Many Catholics, then, thought that in the Waldheim case the pope was being asked to do something not in his job description—to be a civil judge, to pronounce a sentence of guilt on an individual who had not yet had his day in court.

There are, as I see it, continuing problems of perception. For example, Catholics understand the beatification of Edith Stein, or the United Nations' ongoing negative resolutions on Zionism, of which most Catholics are unaware, in a wholly different light from the way Jews perceive these things. But dialogues such as this one can bring us together to enlighten each other on these issues so vital to us.

The Waldheim affair, as I have noted, precipitated a crisis between our two communities. How, Jews felt, could they meet with the pope in Miami in September of 1987 after he had just met with the ex-Nazi Kurt Waldheim? The rumors, later confirmed, were just filtering out at the time. A meeting was arranged between Vatican officials and Jewish leaders in Rome to discuss this urgent question. During the conversation in the offices of the Pontifical Commission for Religious Relations with the Jews in Rome, the deep and always urgent meaning of the genocidal Holocaust for Jews was stressed. The joint press communiqué noted that Nazi ideology, while primarily and uniquely targeted at Jews, also had in it demonic qualities and was profoundly anti-

Christian. Here, as a pastor, I must bear my word of witness to call to mind the Poles, Ukrainians, other Eastern Europeans, and, yes, Germans who also lost relatives or who suffered personally in the Nazi death camps.

At the meeting in Castel Gandolfo on September 1, the pope movingly recalled his statement on the Shoah to the Jews of Warsaw. This, echoed in his letter to Archbishop May and at the meeting with over two hundred national Jewish leaders on September 11 in Miami, helped make Catholics more aware of the significance of the Shoah as something that has touched the Jewish people in such a uniquely painful way and that is freighted with so much meaning for all peoples.

At the meeting at the Vatican on August 31, the Jewish delegates from the United States paid the Catholic Church in the United States great compliments for the way in which we have tried to implement *Nostra Aetate* and combat anti-Semitism. At the same time, to the surprise of some of our partners in dialogue, we pointed out areas in which we have experienced the pain of anti-Catholicism: Catholics, like Jews, were denied jobs and refused housing in many places, and there were also the election campaigns of Al Smith and John F. Kennedy. Even today, I can point to a city in central Pennsylvania where no Catholic sits on the board of a community college. We've seen the negative slant in news reporting on the recent pastoral visit of Pope John Paul II to the United States, with undue emphasis on demonstrations and divisions. In all of the above, and occasionally on TV talk shows and in editorial cartoons as well, the Catholic Church is fair game, with nothing too outrageous to use. We are grateful to the Anti-Defamation League for helping us face these challenges, which Jews know all too well.

Despite the credit given during the Rome meeting to the Church in the United States for working to implement *Nostra Aetate*, my experience in speaking to synagogue and B'nai B'rith groups has been that the Jewish people have not been told of what we have done. Differences between us are highlighted, but our concerted efforts to review and change our textbooks, teaching approaches, and so forth, remain a secret, so far as the lay Jewish community is concerned.

Over and above this, our Catholic schools have been the best instrument for the implementation of *Nostra Aetate* and of other documents from the Holy See and from our U.S. Conference of Catholic Bishops. Studies have shown that the students and graduates of Catholic schools have the most positive attitudes toward people of other religions and races, more so than students in public or private schools. Yet, among our people there is the perception that some Jewish organizations have used the anti-Catholic attitudes associated with the "hard-line separation of Church and state" approach in arguing against aid to students in parochial schools. For example, in the most recent major Supreme Court decision on the issue, carefully constructed federal legislation allowing assistance for remedial instruction to the underprivileged—mostly in the inner cities, where many of the students in Catholic schools are not Catholics and many are members of minority groups—was struck down. The plaintiffs argued for and won a decision striking down this aid, which provided for instruction in secular subjects by public school teachers using public school materials, simply because, it was made to appear, the walls of the classrooms in which the instruction was being given were somehow "infected with Catholicism."

For a Catholic in the United States, there are certain puzzling aspects about the pressure on the Holy See to establish formal diplomatic relations with the State of Israel. You know that we American Catholics have been very supportive of Israel. But American Catholics also know that there were no formal diplomatic relations between the Holy See and the United States itself until about four years ago. At an early stage, when presidents of the United States, such as Harry Truman, suggested a formal exchange of ambassadors, groups such as the American Jewish Congress joined with Protestant groups in opposing it.

As I have listened to concerns expressed to me in meetings in synagogues and B'nai B'rith groups, I have the perception that there is a concern regarding a possible theological reason for the nonestablishment of formal diplomatic ties. It should be very clear that such a concern is based on a fundamental misconception. Pope John Paul II's very clear recognition of the right of Israel to exist, the practical working relations that have already been established with Israel, and the understanding that he has expressed of the State of Israel as a reality—a reality that means a great deal to Jews and that is something rising out of the ashes and sadness of the Holocaust—should go a long way toward helping people in the United States, both Jews and Catholics, see the situation in perspective.

On many occasions in the last few months I have seen in Jewish publications articles as well as letters to the editor that reveal misunderstandings of Catholic positions. For example, I was sent an article from a Jewish publication in Colorado on the beatification of Edith Stein that completely misread the situation. An article from a newspaper in Washington indicated that somehow Christian teaching required a repetition of the "deicide" charge that the Jews were and are collectively guilty of the death of Jesus. Likewise, materials proposed for a Holocaust curriculum in New Jersey contain points that are not only misinformed but could be judged to be anti-Catholic and likely to encourage anti-Catholic attitudes.

I must refer to the recent interview with Cardinal Joseph Ratzinger, the head of the Holy See's Congregation for the Doctrine of the Faith, which attracted media attention in November. The incident showed that we have a system that is beginning to work but also that communications are not yet perfect.

When Rabbi Mordecai Waxman of the Synagogue Council of America telephoned me to say that a [troubling] article had appeared in some Catholic diocesan newspapers regarding an interview given many months earlier by Cardinal Ratzinger, Dr. Eugene Fisher of our Washington office, at my request, immediately contacted the Secretariat for Religious Relations with the Jews in Rome. No one there was even aware of the interview, which had appeared in a relative obscure weekly magazine. Within two days we had by telephone the Secretariat's assurance that Cardinal Ratzinger was unhappy with the printed report, which did not reflect his mind accurately. By the following week there came a copy of the original published article, which dealt mainly with another topic, and an explicit statement pointing out an error in the transcription of the interview and stating his own thought, fully in accord with the official documents of our Church.

As I said to Rabbi Waxman at the time of his initial call, we should not jump to conclusions based upon excerpts taken out of context in interviews. What we depend on is the official text. I know that some still express concern about the original statement, but that understandable concern relates to issues not yet resolved and which we in our Church may take a long while to work through. After all, Saint Paul's writing has certain ambiguities. These are difficult to resolve when he is not around to answer questions!

This leads me to a practical proposal. Could the Anti-Defamation League consider cosponsoring with us a seminar for editors of Jewish and Catholic publications? Such a conference could be addressed by speakers familiar with the principal sensitive issues associated with Jewish-Catholic relations. Jewish editors would learn, and Catholic editors would be reminded of, the enormous internal changes that have taken place within the Catholic Church in terms of seminary and other educational programs. Catholic editors could be helped to see better the Jewish perspective on such topics as the Holocaust and the State of Israel. Such a program would introduce the editors to one another as well, and help build some new and positive bridges between our two communities.

Palm Beach, Florida, February 12, 1988

[Editor's note: The seminar did take place and did have the desired results.]

3
Introducing Elie Wiesel at Notre Dame College

I participate in this evening's program with a sense of deep privilege. In 1978, I heard Elie Wiesel speak as part of a religious observance of the bicentennial of the American Declaration of Independence at a program in Philadelphia. Memories of that evening are still with me, Mr. Wiesel. But before I present you to the audience, I should like to present this community to you and to say a word about the historic moment in which we live.

You come to Maryland, where my predecessor, Cardinal Shehan, was an active leader in helping the Second Vatican Council, a quarter of a century ago, chart for the Catholic Church a renewal in its relationship with the Jewish people, a commitment to ensure that Christian Scripture and teaching be understood and interpreted in proper context and never, ever again be used by anyone in our worldwide faith community as an excuse for anti-Semitism or worse. Rather, the Council directed our Church toward dialogue, the building-up of mutual respect, and the fostering of common efforts for the common good.

You come to a city where, thanks to the Institute for Christian-Jewish Studies, strides exemplary for this area and indeed for this nation have been taken in the promotion of Jewish-Christian understanding for the benefit of the whole community.

You come, Mr. Wiesel, to a city blessed with a large Jewish community and a large Polish-American group as well. Among the latter are some who also share personal memories of years of pain when they, too, were victims, along with a pride that so many of their land are honored among the "righteous Gentiles" at Yad Vashem in Israel.

And to all I say this: we meet in an extraordinary hour in modern history, when most people in Eastern Europe are experiencing a new and living hope for freedom of religion for all, freedom of movement, freedom from fear—all of this undreamt of, even just months ago. It is a time both to thank God and also to entertain concerns for so much that is yet uncertain, perhaps clouded by some peril not clearly seen.

In this context I wish to mention one other person who, like our speaker this evening, has been able to touch and move the human spirit. He is the son of Poland, Karol Wotyła, who eleven years ago was called to Rome to the See of the Apostle Peter. Six years ago at dinner, he spoke to some of us from the United States about East-West tensions, and he thanked us for our bishops' letter on the challenge of peace. But, he said, "The way to peace will come when people of faith in Eastern Europe can raise their voices once again." Meanwhile, even as our speaker this evening has helped much of the world to see the unspeakable horror of the Shoah, so Pope John Paul II has brought to members of the Catholic Church and to many others strong personal leadership in conveying a sense of the uniquely genocidal quality of the Holocaust for Jews.

Two years ago, on the exact anniversary date of the German invasion of Poland, Pope John Paul II met with Jewish and Catholic leaders at his summer home in Castel Gandolfo. After some lengthy discussion of current questions, the pope recalled the Second World War and the Holocaust, telling us how, after the war, he returned to his native town and found empty the homes of his Jewish friends and schoolmates who had perished in the Shoah. He recalled his own spontaneous words to the Jewish community of

Warsaw: the Holocaust is a lesson not only for Jews and Christians but for all humanity. He underscored the unique genocidal quality of those evil days for Jews and reflected on it in the light of the lesson taught by the Exodus, how God can draw good out of evil.[1] On the way back to the city, Doctor Gerhard Reigner, possibly the first to alert the world in 1942 to the reality of the Final Solution, told us insistently that "the pope does understand."

The spirit that thirsts for freedom, for justice, and for peace, the spirit that literally took its cue in Poland from the words and person of Pope John Paul II in his visits there, has now filled and changed that land and spilled over its borders to help accelerate the *perestroika* of Eastern Europe. That spirit, however, has not yet touched Romania, the country of our speaker's birth.

For the gift of Elie Wiesel to our whole world, I give thanks. Unforgettable for me is his eloquent and haunting message of years ago. With that blessing go others: his incisive and challenging writing and his ability to articulate the human conscience to many who have never heard a conscience speak. It is the conscience seared by experiences almost beyond capturing in human speech. Because of this, it was easy for me to join many others in recommending Mr. Wiesel for the Nobel Peace Prize several years ago. He comes to us this evening, now a Nobel Laureate, the recipient of more than eighty awards, a member of many boards, an author of at least fifteen books and numerous articles, and, above all, what the *Washington Post* described as "a symbol, a banner, and a beacon, perhaps *the* survivor of the Holocaust."

Zahor is the Hebrew word to remember, to help *us* remember and not forget that Mr. Wiesel comes to discuss with us the "Imperative for Religious Understanding."

With an enormous sense of honor, I present Mr. Elie Wiesel.

Baltimore, December 7, 1989

13

4
Twenty-Five Years after
Nostra Aetate
The State of Catholic-Jewish Relations

*An Address to the Rabbinical Assembly of
Conservative Judaism*[1]

I begin by paraphrasing something that Rabbi Mordecai Waxman said to us in Rome in 1987: "If you wish to be our friend, you must know what pains us, what causes us pain and hurt." Then and in many subsequent meetings, we Catholics heard what causes pain to our Jewish sisters and brothers. In the spirit of mutuality, we have tried to speak of some of the pain that we have felt as well. As Rabbi Waxman and I have reminded each other and our audiences on many occasions, we learned also that we speak in different ways, out of different cultures and histories, out of different philosophical, theological, and educational backgrounds. It is not always simply a question of what we believe, but also how we couch our thoughts and feelings. I have often said to Rabbi Waxman that his way of speech is more direct, his choice of language more robust. I speak out of a background in which I was educated in our schools and, by the blessings of providence, in the discussions of the Second Vatican Council.

14

This Council produced the document *Nostra Aetate*, which governs the inner renewal of our teaching and preaching in ways to encourage more positive attitudes toward Judaism as a living religion, to build bridges of dialogue in which we sit at the table as peers, as partners, and to help us as Catholics to appreciate the Jewish context of the Christian Scriptures, as well as the Jewish roots of Jesus, his people, and the infant Church.

We need first to talk about those things that cause us pain. From exchanges we've had over the years, I have been careful to tell Catholic friends that for Jews the Holocaust, in all its horrors, was uniquely genocidal. In interpreting this to Catholics, I use the analogy of *sacrament*. For us a sacrament is a sacred sign in which God works, and anything that would detract from that sign or show disrespect for it is sacrilege. And so I say to Catholics, for Jewish people sensitive to the Holocaust and all its horrors, anything that might seem to lessen its significance is sacrilegious and will cause pain and painful reactions.

In our meeting in Rome in 1987, we reflected together in the final communiqué on the demonic ideology that spawned the Holocaust. We understood it as anti-religious and mourned together the many Catholics who perished in the death camps along with the Jews. We know what happened in Holland, to go back a bit into history to underscore a particular moment of the Holocaust. In 1942, the Catholic bishops of Holland protested the roundup of the Jews. In retaliation, the Nazis sent to Auschwitz the Catholics of Jewish descent first. And they hastened the deportation of all the Jews.

Even today it is not clear how much good such precise public denunciations in other settings would have accomplished in the face of that dictatorship with total power in its hands. As you know, even in the Jewish community at the time there existed a dilemma, with some Jews deciding not to speak out publicly but, rather, to work quietly behind the scenes. Today, both the Jewish and the Catholic communities need to grapple with the complexities of that tragic period, not in a judgmental way but constructively, for the sake of the future. *Memoria futuri*—remembering for the sake of the future.

Perceptions of the Holocaust continue to surface as points of difference. For example, we witness the experience that came to a head last summer and fall with respect to a convent situated near the Auschwitz death camp. News stories told us first of a meeting that had taken place in February of 1987. Jewish leaders in Europe met with four cardinals, including Cardinal Macharsky, the archbishop of Krakow, to discuss their concerns regarding the presence of a Carmelite monastery adjacent to the death camps at Auschwitz-Birkenau. The cardinals and other Catholics involved in the discussion came to see the sensitivity of the issue, and they worked with the Jewish leaders toward a solution that would be positive and forward-looking. Together they committed themselves not simply to relocating the site of the convent—to characterize it in this way would be to distort the understanding that was reached. Rather, they looked toward the construction, at a distance from the camp, of a center intended to foster Catholic-Jewish relations through study, discussion, and prayer. When we come to the mission of prayer now, we know that it is a concept not familiar to many contemporary ears. The Carmelite nuns, whose life is dedicated to prayer and contemplation, would have an honored role. Their convent would be situated in the context of this new center.

Then came the complications. We know a few of them. For example, for at least a year the Polish government would not issue the necessary permits. This can be understood in the light of a report I heard that it was not uncommon in Communist Poland for the construction of a new public building to take seven years. So the declaration signed by the Catholic parties was not a realistic promise in terms of the actual situation then prevailing in Poland. (Now times have changed because the government has changed.)

The rest is history: the violation of the cloister and the clamorous demonstrations on the convent grounds by Rabbi Avi Weiss and his associates; the harsh physical reactions of some Polish workers on the scene; the escalation, the demonstrations, and the reactions finally involving statements by Church leaders in Poland and elsewhere. On September 19, 1987, the president of the Holy See's Commission for Religious Relations with the Jews, Cardinal Johannes Willebrands, issued a statement on behalf of the Holy See. He commended the stand of the Polish Bishops' Commission on Judaism, which had been made public earlier in the month, a stand committing the Church to the new center. He reaffirmed Pope John Paul II's commendation of the proposal given a year earlier, adding this time the pledge of financial help. Within a few days, following several meetings with Jewish leaders in Poland and England, Cardinal Glemp announced his personal support of the project, and the matter moved from the front pages. In February of this year, work was begun on the new center—as a step favored by the return of greater freedom from government control in Poland.

Toward the end of the public discussions, many voices of Jews, Catholics, and observers were raised in favor of restraint and reason in dialogue. These voices helped establish the needed atmosphere. And even as, through the discussions, Catholics were reminded afresh of deep Jewish sensitivity regarding the Holocaust, I am hopeful that our Jewish partners in dialogue gained some new insight into the pains that were felt in the Catholic community, particularly in our Polish Catholic community.

Our Jewish friends learned, for example, what may strike many visitors to the Yad Vashem Holocaust Memorial in Israel— that the most numerous of all on the list of the righteous Gentiles who risked their lives to help Jews are Polish Catholics. They also learned that the death camp at Auschwitz was built first to handle the Polish intellectual elite, including the clergy and army officers who still survived. These selected Poles were being exterminated at Auschwitz a full year and more before the horrifying decision was taken to try to eliminate the Jews. And perhaps our Jewish friends have learned as well that within the Catholic Church there is now and has always been a great deal of variety, flexibility, and disagreement. I have to explain to Catholics that the American Jewish Congress, the World Jewish Congress, and the American Jewish Committee are three separate organizations that do not always share identical viewpoints. And to Jewish friends I must say that within the Catholic Church there are many different juridical entities, some of which possess by Church law an autonomy that you might find surprising. I apply this especially to Carmelite monasteries. One of the interesting documents that I have in our own archives in Baltimore records the welcome that our first bishop, John Carroll, extended two hundred years ago to the first community of nuns to arrive in the United States. They were Carmelites. Shortly after their arrival he wrote them several times asking them to undertake a specific task of education. Each time they responded, specifically rejecting the invitation to work in that field. They had and they have a great deal of autonomy. A bishop has the role of ensuring that the liturgy is celebrated properly and that certain rules are observed. But beyond that, canon law affords nuns a great deal of autonomy in making decisions about such things as to how they are going to build their house, where they build it, and how they organize it inside.

The stage is set this fall for a meeting in Prague between the International Jewish Committee for Interreligious Understanding and the Holy See's Commission for Religious Relations with the Jews. We shall discuss something that we have been looking forward to for several years, the implications of the Shoah, in this constructive fashion: Catholic scholars and Jewish scholars will sit down and talk about those tragic days, and in the process assist the Holy See's Commission to begin to prepare its own document on the Holocaust and the study of the history of anti-Semitism.

The next question I want to talk about is this: Why does the Holy See not have full diplomatic relations with the State of Israel? At our meeting in Rome, the representatives of the

Vatican's Secretariat of State spoke of serious and unresolved problems in the region. For the same reasons, the Holy See does not have an exchange of ambassadors with the Kingdom of Jordan, so it is *not*, as one sometimes hears, a situation of judgments uniquely directed toward Israel. The unsettled situation is now symbolized very dramatically in the ongoing uprising (intifada), over the answer to the "Palestinian Question" (for which the Holy See does not hold Israel solely responsible; clearly there is the responsibility of the Arab states who helped create the situation and it is going to take a joint action to resolve it). In addition, there are also concerns and fears regarding the situation of Catholic minorities in Muslim countries and a hope for an international guarantee for the full religious rights of all the major faith groups in Jerusalem, something that is again in the picture with the current question of the Hospice of Saint John of Jerusalem.

Regarding the hospice, I told Rabbi Waxman that when I read Cardinal John O'Connor's statement, I thought that he was learning Mordy's direct, robust way of speaking. There is a dimension to the controversy that is not fully visible here in the United States, just as with the Auschwitz-Carmel controversy before last summer. Then there was an issue of burning concern in Europe, of which we were a bit aware here, but it was not our issue. When Cardinal O'Connor wrote last week, he was sharing with our community and with our partners in dialogue the enormous sense of pain within the Christian community in Jerusalem. The following is a response written this week by Dr. Eugene Fisher, a dear friend of many of us, our staff person for Catholic-Jewish relations for the U.S. Conference of Catholic Bishops in Washington, who has worked with Rabbi Waxman and was part of our meeting in Rome two years ago:

> More recent statements such as that by the Israeli government seeking to justify the action have tended to

escalate the issue even as it is being adjudicated. The question now seems to be a rhetorical tussle over how to frame the issue. The Israeli government, and yours as well if I read you correctly, seem [to believe]...that the problem with the takeover lies only with its manner and timing, and it therefore does not raise any fundamental issues of the *status quo* of the rights of the Christian community in Jerusalem. The reasoning behind this is, as the communiqué from the Israeli embassy put it, that the buildings in question are neither a church nor a holy site of any kind and are not used for religious worship. They are owned by the Greek Orthodox Patriarchate and in the past served as a hospital. The issue of definition is, I believe, crucial to understanding the varied reactions of the Jewish and Christian communities at the present stage of the crisis. If one accepts the above definition, then our own feeling that the Christian response has been an overreaction is quite understandable. On the other hand, it needs to be clear that Christians by and large do not accept this definition of the issue, that the problem lies solely with the manner and timing of the takeover itself. Christians in Jerusalem and in the United States perceive the issue precisely as a threat to the rights of religious minorities in Jerusalem.[2]

Last summer, as we visited in Jerusalem with Christian leaders—Catholic, Orthodox, and Anglican—and with their people, we found many who felt that their rights were imperiled. This is not a new issue, but one that has been festering for many years. They see it as a curtailment of traditional Christian rights not only to have free access to the holy places but to be allowed to live unmolested alongside our sacred Christian shrines. Dr. Fisher continued:

Whether currently in use as a hostel or not, that building is a place where pilgrims travelling to pray at the holy sites may stay, and Christians see St. John's Hospice as very much a necessary extension of the Church of the Holy Sepulchre itself. Manifestly the Greek Orthodox Church does not want this site to be put to the use to which the settlers want to put it. Equally manifestly the settlers and those within the Israeli government who aided them know perfectly well that what they were doing would violate the will of the owner of the property, as their manner and timing reveal. If one accepts the way in which Israeli Christians must perceive the issues, then their reactions do become understandable, since for them it touches on the survival of the Christian community of Israel. If even property connected with essential Christian holy places, property once used and perhaps to be used again for a strictly religious purpose, housing pilgrims as the name and the religious symbols on the buildings signify, can be taken over in this way with the active cooperation of the Israeli government, then what recourse will there be in the future? You may say that the local Christians in Jerusalem were incorrect in their assessment of what is at stake. You may be right. But you are unlikely to convince them or us of the correctness of your moderating assessment. The matter has already escalated beyond the point where technical discussions about whether the hospice is a religious site or not are even relevant. To Christians it is a religious site, nor can arguments, however brilliant, from outside the Greek Orthodox community convince Christians that it is not what the Greek Orthodox say it is. It is their right and theirs alone to determine what is or is not religious for them.[3]

So, you see, the issue for the Christians in Jerusalem and around the world is a very, very sensitive one, in a real sense an "Auschwitz convent" in reverse. The takeover took place in the holiest of times near the holiest of Christian shrines, and the police response included knocking down the Greek Orthodox Patriarch and also tussling with the Latin Rite Patriarch. Such actions did not help clarify or calm feelings in the Christian community or anywhere these reports have reached. This is an area where it is good for us that we can talk, and not just depend on news reports.

Lake Kiamesha, New York, May 21, 1990

[Editor's note: The situation with the Hospice of Saint John of Jerusalem was ultimately resolved.]

5
Union of American Hebrew Congregations

I feel quite at home among you and trust that you feel the same here in Baltimore, a city in a state founded as a refuge for Catholics persecuted elsewhere in the colonies for their beliefs. The Union of American Hebrew Congregations (UAHC),[1] representing Reform Judaism, has long been in the forefront of interreligious dialogue within the religious Jewish community. We note with gratitude the fact that UAHC alone among Jewish religious organizations has a full-time office in this field, with whose representatives the U.S. Conference of Catholic Bishops has worked fruitfully over the years on a wide variety of significant projects.

One could mention many such joint activities. Here, it may suffice to recall the excellent joint study guide on our Catholic Bishops' Peace Pastoral,[2] coauthored by Eugene Fisher of our Secretariat for Ecumenical and Interreligious Affairs and by the late Annette Daum, distinguished predecessor of Rabbi Gary Breton-Granatoor. Such joint efforts on the serious and sensitive social issues of our times illustrate what is possible for us to accomplish in and for society when we work together to study and confront these issues. We also need to remember what is possible on the different levels on which we engage each other in dialogue, whether international, national, or local. Rabbi Bretton-

Granatoor and I, for example, along with Eugene Fisher, were present in September 1990 at the meeting in Prague of the International Catholic-Jewish Liaison Committee, which offered so much hope and basis for constructive progress in Catholic-Jewish relations throughout the world and especially in Eastern Europe.

On the national level within the United States, we have various forums of dialogue and cooperation, ranging from our excellent long-range relations with such Jewish agencies as the American Jewish Committee to a formal, twice-yearly consultation with the Synagogue Council of America, of which UAHC forms one of six constituent members. These consultations have great potential for furthering our relations. There are as well opportunities for joint theological studies with Jewish agencies and with the UAHC that are not available to us within the framework of our consultation with the Synagogue Council of America,[3] as we have discovered also with regard to the National Workshops on Christian-Jewish Relations. We have a rich variety of ways to relate to one another, despite the difficulties we may sometimes have in probing beneath the surface to understand truly and fully each other's perspectives and deepest motivations.

As we meet, we remember that a week from tomorrow marks the anniversary of *Kristallnacht*, the night of shattered glass and burning synagogues that marked the opening of the Shoah. We remember with pain and with prayer the victims of what a representative of the U.S. Catholic bishops, speaking at the time on national radio, called "a shameless orgy of ruthless oppression, even extinction, willed by the mad lust for power…upon a helpless, already shackled people."[4] We know that even as we meet today in better times, the dark shadow of the horror that was begun that night may still cast a pall over our dialogue.

The Holocaust and its lingering shadow have been at the heart of the controversies between our two communities in the summers of 1987, 1989, and 1991. Today, I am encouraged by the knowledge

that our structures of dialogue in this country, which might have seemed frail in contrast to the difficulties to be faced, not only survived but, I believe, have been made firmer by the testing they have undergone. Here I must say that the Interreligious Affairs Committee of UAHC and its staff have been, during these difficult periods, a bulwark of strength and support for the seemingly innocuous but in truth highly controversial notion that dialogue and understanding, rather than confrontation and press releases, are the path to progress in our relationship.

Within this rather broad framework geographically and historically sketched above, please allow me to raise just a few concerns from the Catholic side of the dialogue that might fruitfully be explored between us.

First, I would like to raise consideration of our joint statement with the Synagogue Council of America (SCA), "A Lesson of Value: A Joint Statement on Moral Education in the Public Schools." This statement, which is very supportive of public education, noted with some irony that

> in recent years, there has been a growing reluctance to teach values in our public educational system out of a fear that children might be indoctrinated with a specific religious belief....[Yet] values like honesty, compassion, integrity, tolerance, loyalty, and belief in human worth and dignity are embedded in our respective religious traditions and in the civic fabric of our society....We are convinced that, even apart from the content of a specific faith, it is possible to teach these shared values.

Given the nature of American public education, a vision such as this one, which we were able to articulate jointly with representatives of the SCA, can be implemented effectively only through local school boards across the country. This is a challenge that, while nationally formulated, can perhaps best be met on the congregational—parish to synagogue—level, so well represented here today.

Second, linked to the understanding that there are some commonly held values necessary for the preservation of a civilized society that can be articulated and asserted in the most pluralistic of settings is a consideration of the question of pornography. Obviously, there are a number of First Amendment issues involved, concerns I would share and support. But even after the most scrupulous attendance to these issues, there remain some rather large areas of shared concern on which we can speak together, such as we are beginning to discuss with the SCA. Child pornography comes immediately to mind, as does the related issue of the exploitation, indeed virtual enslavement, of some women involved in the process of producing pornography. More investigation and joint reflection, I urge, is necessary to combat such evil practices.

Third, there is the consideration of rethinking the issue of aid to non–public school students and parents, as constitutionally appropriate, with a focus on aid to the needy, not on specific institutions, whether religious or secular. A number of arguments from the common good might be considered in such a rethinking, ranging from acknowledgment of the primacy of parental responsibility and the consequent necessity of respecting their freedom of choice, to the affirmation of pluralism as opposed to governmental monopoly of education that lies at the heart of the issue.

In addition to this rethinking, a special note with regard to Catholic-Jewish understandings can be added. Surveys have shown that graduates of Catholic schools are more positive toward Jews and Judaism than other Catholics or the general population. There are approximately 9,500 primary and secondary Catholic schools serving over 3 million students, although the large majority of Catholic youth are educated in the public school system, which explains our great interest in maintaining strong public schools. But if one is serious about the full implementation of *Nostra Aetate* and subsequent Church documents, one must acknowledge the key role that must be played by our schools. Thus, a reconsideration of this has the potential for greatly enhancing the common good of the nation, of the children, and of all our efforts at interreligious amity.

The fourth area of consideration relates to a topic that I understand you are taking up in your own bioethics committee. This is the issue of euthanasia, which is quite distinct from the issue of termination of medical treatment. Here one is dealing with the active intervention by a medical professional through lethal injection or other means for the purpose of ending a human life. Such laws as are now being considered in Washington State raise these issues for all religious communities, perhaps especially for us Jews and Catholics, who have such a traditional commitment to and involvement in the medical professions, hospitals, and so forth.

Finally, I would raise from our point of view as American Catholics our quite natural concerns for the Christian minority in Israel and the occupied territories. I do not do this in any sense of making charges against the Israeli government. Rather, mine is a plea for greater understanding, empathy, and support for a dwindling community witnessing to Christian faith in what we Christians have for centuries termed the "Holy Land." The Arab Christian community is a minority within a minority and hence doubly vulnerable. It does things and has sensitivities that the larger communities surrounding it may find difficult to understand but that are quite coherent from its own point of view.

One such issue is the takeover of the Hospice of Saint John of Jerusalem, now in the courts. The statements of the UAHC at the time of the takeover were commendable and are remembered by our bishops with gratitude. This emboldens me to ask for even more (perhaps a bit of the celebrated chutzpah has rubbed off on me through all these years of dialogue). I would ask our American Jewish colleagues to continue to pester their Israeli

Jewish colleagues for resolution of this issue and for greater sensitivity on related issues involving Christians, especially in the occupied territories where the difficulties are most acute.

Again, this is not a matter of charges or of "rights" or of politics or even the macro-issues of the Middle East peace process, for which we all pray. Rather, it is a matter of sensitivity and doing perhaps a bit more than is owed in a given situation because that is the nature of a living relationship between two ancient peoples of faith in a world still broken. We need together to begin to take the steps necessary to enable us better to work together toward *tikkun olam*—the mending of our world.

Baltimore, November 1, 1991

6
National Jewish Community Relations Advisory Council

In expressing my deep appreciation for this invitation, I note that we are gathering not long after the fourteenth meeting of the International Catholic-Jewish Liasion Committee—which is the link between the Holy See and the International Jewish Committee for Interreligious Consultations—a meeting that was held for the first time ever in the Western Hemisphere in Baltimore last May, building on the Prague declaration. For the Catholic Church in Eastern Europe, there is the enormous challenge of rebuilding infrastructure (churches, schools, seminaries, offices). The Church must also locate and care for so many who have been dislocated. In the Asian parts of the former Soviet Union, there are hundreds of thousands of Catholics scattered in the Gulag who need immediate help to survive.

The timely meeting of the liaison committee in Prague in September 1990 helped us move on two fronts: for the long term, material for the Church's internal document on the Holocaust, an effort continued in Baltimore last May; for the short term, commitment to work at stopping anti-Semitism, defined as a sin against God and humanity, in Eastern and Central Europe. In December 1991, the special assembly of the Synod of Bishops for Europe made a forceful declaration opposing anti-Semitism, and the Polish Bishops' Conference issued a most helpful and aggressive statement with a strong call to combat anti-Semitism. Further steps came in the last few months when Bishop Lehmann, president of the German Bishops' Conference, spoke in the name of his conference and in that of Pope John Paul II condemning the new manifestations of anti-Semitism in Germany and elsewhere.

When I began to prepare for this meeting, I thought it helpful to distinguish between "recurring tensions" and "immediate challenges." But as I wrote, I found these closely linked. As I speak of the Middle East and the advance of a process that we hope will bring genuine peace to the region at last, trying to capture a complex range of issues in a few words, I speak of a group that is often forgotten, the Christian minority. About 110,000 in Israel and 60,000 in the territories, who have been there for centuries, now feel under siege.

On a visit to Israel early last year, Cardinal O'Connor of New York pointed out to representatives of the Israeli government, the Arab states, and the Palestinians that Catholics look for three steps on the way to peace: the resolution of the "Palestinian Question" and peaceful relations with her neighbors; the assurance of security for Christians throughout the Middle East; and recognized guarantees for access to the holy places in Jerusalem for people of all faiths and equal rights there for peoples of all faiths. Cardinal O'Connor has indicated the need for greater sensitivity on the part of the Israeli government. Latin Rite Patriarch Michel Sabbah,[1] for example, speaks out on behalf of the Palestinian Christians who are experiencing any injustices. Many have criticized him for this. Cardinal O'Connor and others have urged that there be meetings between officials in the Israeli government and the Patriarch so that there might be better understanding.

On a personal note, I am indebted to Patriarch Sabbah for much hospitality during our 1989 visit. Both publicly and privately, he has expressed himself in favor of a peaceful settlement.

His 1990 pastoral letter "Pray for the Peace of Jerusalem"[2] stands as a classic document, calling his own people to respect the place of the State of Israel and to love their Jewish brothers and sisters.

In the positive context created by the peace process, the State of Israel and the Holy See have formed a joint commission moving toward full and continuing diplomatic relations. We recognize that there will be ups and downs in the peace process, which we should accompany with our prayers. Ordinary people—Israelis and Palestinians; Jews, Christians, and Muslims—are suffering, and they hunger for a peace that will let them raise their children without fear...a peace that will leave Israel free and secure, and the Palestinians with their own homeland at last and with a sense that their basic human dignity is acknowledged.

The background and context of all of this, of course, is the Shoah. At the Prague and Baltimore meetings of the International Christian-Jewish Liaison Committee, we looked at painful years, hearing witnesses to the Shoah describe days of unspeakable horror, devilish betrayal, and undreamed-of heroism. We were looking at episodes of human courage and weakness, not fearing to listen to descriptions of the failure of Christians, nor failing to give credit to those whose courage saved lives, often at the risk, often at the cost, of their own.

While we may still look for more clarity in the Holy See's policy with respect to certain specific events during the Nazi years, generalizations that would allege a total lack of action on the part of the Church or the "silence" of Pope Pius XII miss the mark. During the war, editorials in the *New York Times* praised the pope's public statements, which were clearly understood as condemning the racist policies of Nazi Germany. In May of 1943, the U.S. press reported on Nazi reactions to the pope's position: "Pope Pius XII has condemned the principles of the totalitarian state, has rejected racism and has forbidden all Catholics to participate in the anti-Jewish campaigns....The Church has rejected the hand offered to her [by Germany]. May she bear the responsibility for this in the annals of history."

There is no question that some Christian leaders failed, nor is there a question that others acted heroically. Clearly, the policies of the Holy See contributed to the rescue of many. Last summer I had the privilege of visiting Poland on an extremely intense and useful mission. Jerome Chanes, and rabbis Jack Bemporad, Jim Rudin, and Leon Klenicki, were among some twenty Jewish leaders who, with half a dozen Catholics, visited scenes of suffering and discussed ways to bring hope to the future. A long meeting, ably chaired by Archbishop Henryk Muszyński, was held with the Polish Bishops' Commission on Judaism, at which we heard Dr. Stanislaw Krajewski, a Polish Jewish scholar, lift up a basic problem today. He said: "In the United States, most of the Holocaust survivors are Jewish; in Poland, most are Catholics. Each group has its own memories and has difficulty when it hears reports of the others' memories from a distance."

Our "traveling dialogue" had its most poignant moments at the concentration camps of Auschwitz and Birkenau, where the two Jewish survivors in our group, a married couple, by chance met a Polish Catholic survivor who now resides in the United States. The woman's survival was made possible by another Polish Catholic who was a friend of the person we met at Auschwitz. An afternoon at the new center at Osweicim (incidentally, the new convent has been completed after three years of building in a difficult economic climate) and a visit to the shrine of the Black Madonna at Czestochowa the next day gave us a close-up look at the religious side of Polish Catholic devotional life. It helped us understand Polish reactions to what they saw as a desecration of the sacred precincts of the convent and why, as Archbishop Muszyński noted, the cross near the convent, outside the actual death camp, has a special symbolism for Catholic Poles. Within two months of the Nazi invasion in 1939, Polish Catholic leaders, including more than half the priests of some dioceses, were arrested—some summarily executed, others sent to places like Auschwitz, where most subsequently died.

During this trip, the Jewish delegation presented a plan whereby American Jewish scholars would be invited to make presentations on Jewish history and spirituality in Polish seminaries. I discussed this proposal in a meeting in August with Cardinal Glemp and the executive committee of the Polish Bishops' Conference. Subsequently the entire conference adopted the proposal, which will be implemented this year. Last summer our delegation also said that parallel steps must be taken in the United States and elsewhere to offer Polish Catholic scholars an opportunity to present to key Jewish groups facts of Polish history and of the Nazi days to overcome the stereotypes of Poles and Catholics that contribute to continued misunderstanding.

Regarding U.S. concerns, I would like to raise once again the need to include Catholic schools, as an affirmation of pluralism as opposed to governmental monopoly of education, among those receiving government assistance in poor areas and the inner cities of this country. Here, I would express my appreciation to the government of Israel, which underwrites up to 85 percent of the operating costs of religious schools, including Catholic schools, in Israel and the territories. The amount of allocation is correlated to the observance of certain quality criteria. The equivalent of more than eight million American dollars was given in direct aid to Catholic schools by Israel in 1991. Israel, like most other democratic countries, has concluded that aid to students benefits the total good of the country rather than detracting from it.

I am most grateful to you for this opportunity to speak with you today, part of a great tradition in your organization and in our nation of ongoing dialogue about issues of common interest.

Beltsville, Maryland, February 15, 1993

7
Israel Bond Rally

I am deeply grateful to Mr. Stuart Greenebaum for the invitation to be with you and for his gracious introduction. It is good to be with you and with so many of you again today. Mr. Greenebaum brings alive some memories that have helped shape his own sense of self and of history. His words inspire me to share a few as well.

My Catholic bishop had asked me to represent the Diocese of Harrisburg at a rally on the banks of the Susquehanna River. Rabbi Jerry Wolpe of Beth El spoke movingly, unforgettably, as he evoked the history of the Jewish people: their suffering, their sense of abandonment, the full horrors of the Holocaust, and their hope now embodied in the State of Israel—and how at that moment again they seemed to stand alone. I also spoke at the rally, bringing the sentiments and prayers of Catholic neighbors for those who with us shared ties of faith to a land that, because so many call it holy, should also be a place of peace. In a special way I remember offering prayers for the relatives of many present who were in Israel, to study or to offer assistance, of whom no news was available. I remember telling Bishop Leech about the daughter of Rabbi David Silver, who had not been heard from, and how he immediately sent a handwritten note expressing his concern and prayer to the rabbi, a dear friend as well as a leader to many in the area. I recall the day in September twenty years later, September 1, 1987, when we were at Castel Gandolfo. Pope John Paul II spoke of his meditation that morning—the meaning of the Exodus—and how, out of the ashes of the Holocaust, Israel stood before the world as a symbol of the hope of the Jewish people, and how the memory of the Holocaust itself was a warning to Christians, and indeed all others on this planet, of an evil never to be repeated.

We all know how the pope in many ways—for example, last year in the Holocaust Concert in the Vatican and especially through his best-selling book[1]—has opened his heart to the world, repeating the message he shared with us in 1987. In these recent years, your Catholic neighbors here and across our country have been joined with you in prayer for the peace process that has now begun. We pray for a peace that will keep Israel secure and honor Palestinian dignity, a peace that will let families of the region raise their children in a climate from which fear at last is banished.

To you who live here in Baltimore and in the greater metropolitan area, I want to express a word of thanks on behalf of your Catholic neighbors for the lessons that you give us in your generosity toward all that is good in our community: the arts, education, health care, social services—all these have benefited because of your goodness and your leadership.

The other day Dr. Art Abrahamson called me about the press reports on Father Henryk Jankowski's statement in the presence of Lech Wałesa.[2] I told him how quickly the Polish Catholic Church reacted. My friend, Bishop Tadeusz Pieronek, secretary general of the Polish Bishops' Conference, instantly branded Father Jankowski's remarks as "irresponsible talk." Bishop Stanislaw Gadecki, chair of the Polish Bishops' Commission for Dialogue with the Jews, our guest here in Baltimore three years ago, issued a five-paragraph statement repudiating the remarks and pointing out how the Church must work to overcome evil with good. Archbishop Tadeusz Goclowski, archbishop of Gdansk, when asked to comment, expressed his opposition to what had been said and apologized for the statement. More recently, Father Remi Hoeckman[3] of the Holy See's Commission for Religious Relations with the Jews supported the statements made by these Polish bishops.

I want to say a personal word about that statement in which the loyalty of all Jews in Poland was questioned by the preacher. In past generations, American Catholics have felt the sting in having their loyalty to America called into question because of our religious faith and ancestral heritages. We know from our own history how painful that can be. Any voice that spreads systematic mistrust, suspicion, and even contempt must be repudiated.

Against the background of troubling news, there is also good news. A story in the *Baltimore Sun* yesterday troubled many of us. I was troubled because I knew that the real story was good news, not bad news for Catholic-Jewish relations. My predecessor Cardinal Shehan helped the Holy See develop notes[4] published by the Holy See in 1974 to guide preachers and teachers in correcting misimpressions given when portions of the New Testament, especially in the Gospel of John, are taken out of context. I chaired our national committee that deals with interreligious issues when, here in the United States, we prepared a document to apply this teaching to our own country.[5] For years the Archdiocese of Baltimore has been a national pioneer in helping its priests and teachers, and those preparing to teach, understand that Judaism is a living faith.

We still make mistakes and we are still learning from each other as we continue to develop our interreligious relations. I want to say that the young priest to whom reference was made in the stories yesterday is a fine example of one who is sensitive to this issue and who has faithfully preached according to our principles. I myself have spoken at the Cathedral of Mary Our Queen to remind those who listened to the Gospel of John that the entire infant Christian community was Jewish. Jesus was, as the apostle Paul wrote, a Jew according to the flesh. His mother Mary, the apostles, those who wrote the Gospels—all were Jews. In this context it is clearly understood by those who read and those who listen that those referred to as "Jews" represent just one segment of the population. We are taught again and again by our Scriptures and our Church that Jesus died not because of what a few did long ago, but because in every age of human history people have failed to measure up to the standards of the Law that God gave through Moses. The message of the death of Jesus is not the message of something that calls for any kind of vengeance, but rather it is the sign of God's mercy and love and a call to us to be generous in our love of and service to others.

The purpose of dialogue is to help Christians appreciate Jews and Jews appreciate Christians, and to help them be prepared to try to explain their faith to the other tradition without, however, ever compromising their own. Dialogue is an invitation to be faithful, to deepen understanding, and to find ways to remove misunderstanding and reasons for distrust. Happily, as long as we have the telephone and opportunities like this, I am confident that our relationships, already strong, can grow even stronger.

Last Friday in Vatican City, Archbishop Giovanni Battista Re presided over the planting of a thirty-year-old olive tree that had been sent by the State of Israel. He remarked that a thirty-year-old tree was appropriate because, under divine providence, thirty years have passed since the Second Vatican Council ushered in the new era of relations between the Catholic Church and the world Jewish family. In these thirty years, so much has been accomplished.

I am aware that many years ago Cardinal Shehan purchased an Israel Bond as a sincere and significant sign of hope and trust. I am pleased to announce my intention to do the same, which is coupled with my hope and prayer for God's peace for Israel, for her Palestinian neighbors, and all her neighbors as, please God, a new peace is forged that will be a sign of shalom for all the world. Thank you.

Baltimore, June 22, 1995

8
Lessons to Learn from the Catholic Rescuers

U.S. Holocaust Memorial Museum[1]

In 1990, within a year of the "Velvet Revolution," the International Catholic-Jewish Liaison Committee began in newly liberated Prague a painful but necessary process of healing and reconciliation. This was a joint examination, country by country, of events that took place over a half century ago that today we place under the single, biblical term *Shoah*. Our joint examination of data and memory began with a visit to Theresienstadt—a major holding place for Jews being sent to the death camps—a place where many did in fact die because of disease and the wretched living conditions there, although it was briefly a "showpiece" used to deceive the Red Cross into believing that the inmates were being treated humanely. Tragically, the world at large believed what it wanted to believe and did what it wanted to do, which was virtually nothing.

Today we celebrate the memory of some non-Jews—specifically Catholics—who did do something at a time of utmost crisis when most European Catholics either could not or would not help their neighbors in desperate need. Our visit to Theresienstadt took place on a dark day, with a gentle rain falling, as if to underscore the sadness of our pilgrimage. When our emotionally drained group returned from Theresienstadt, Cardinal Edward I. Cassidy, president of the Pontifical Commission for Religious Relations with the Jewish People, rose to open the official meeting. What he said furnished a context for our reflections. The Church, he said, can only approach the Shoah in such a place and on such an occasion in a spirit of "repentance/*teshuvah*" for the evil that so many of its baptized members perpetrated and so many others failed to stop.

Similarly, when Pope John Paul II announced his plan for Christian preparation for the Jubilee Year 2000, he called on the Church first to examine its past failings and to acknowledge its need for repentance before God. This sense of repentance, of acknowledgment of the need for Catholic repentance, provides as well the proper context for our own celebration in the capital city of our country. The lives and the saving deeds of the Catholics that we remember here today represent crucially important moral lights in a period of darkness. Our celebration of the brightness of that light and the preciousness of that witness is at once intensified and muted by the poignant awareness that, when all is said and done, they were a relative few among us, and no one can know how many, because some surely perished with those they tried to save.

The stories of the rescuers that we have heard here and read about elsewhere are truly remarkable. One such was Father Bernard Lichtenberg, rector of the Catholic cathedral in Berlin, who defied the German authorities Sunday after Sunday by preaching sermons against Nazism and condemning anti-Semitism and the persecution of Jews. He was picked up by the Gestapo, mistreated, and released. Heroically, he returned to the pulpit to continue his attacks on Nazi atrocities, was picked up again, and died on the way to Dachau. On June 23, 1996, in the context of a papal Mass at the cathedral in Berlin where Lichtenberg preached, Pope John Paul II beatified him, declaring him "blessed," which means someone whose virtuous life and often heroic death by martyrdom make that person worthy of remembrance and veneration by all the world's Catholics—in this case, a model of proper Christian attitude and behavior toward Jews and Judaism.

We have heard also of Polish[2] and Italian[3] nuns, representing others all over Europe, who risked their convents, even the breach of cloister. Indeed, the story of Italy bears remembering. Although at first allied with and then occupied by the Nazis, the Italians saved over 80 percent of their Jewish neighbors. And the Italian army saved thousands of others wherever it could reach them. Many of these stories have been untold until recently, and we remember here today those who have labored to preserve their memory, people like Rabbi Harold Schulweiss, Eva Fleischner, and Sy Rotter—and, of course, that most remarkable of Israeli institutions, Yad Vashem in Jerusalem.

We remember, too, Catholic groups such as the French Catholic resisters who, in opposition to both the Nazis and the collaborationist Vichy government, were led by such figures as Henri de Lubac[4] and who organized to save Jewish lives at the risk of their own. We remember Żegota, a distinctly and uniquely Polish organization, which risked all against unbelievable odds and whose story is told in this museum. Shortly, we will hold a remembrance of the French Carmelite Père Jacques de Jésus,[5] who saved the lives of so many Jewish children, and on whom the museum has assembled a special exhibit.

It has been argued that to try to discern the meaning in, or to derive lessons from, the Holocaust is fruitless at best and perhaps blasphemous. Can we, however, learn from the witness of the righteous? Surely, they can, like the saints, be models for doing the right thing to do in such circumstances. And, just as surely, we Catholics who are teachers need such models if we are to be able to prepare the next generations of Christians properly for living moral lives in a world that can, as it did in the 1940s, descend into absolute moral chaos with dizzying rapidity.

If the righteous are to be our models for the future, we need to learn what the studies teach us about them. First, morality was deeply implanted in the fiber of their being, whether they were sophisticated and had advanced training or, as we would say in Maryland, they were "just folks." They frequently had to make a life-or-death decision on very short notice, perhaps a matter of minutes. From their example we recognize the need for basic moral principles—what is right, what it is wrong—to become deeply embedded in our consciousness today, which is a lesson for public education no less than for private or religious education.

Second, the righteous had a deep sense that there was ultimate meaning to life beyond the present. While their separate under-standings of that meaning may have varied, their experience reminds us of the need to place our lives in a wider context of human meaning and interrelatedness. We will hardly have the inner resources to respond to difficult moral challenges in our own day if we are only living for the present—if we are not open to the tran-scendent dimension with all that it tells us about God and about our human pilgrimage through history. This underscores the critical importance of faith in God.

Third, many of the righteous had a prior acquaintance with Jews, though not necessarily with the people they actually rescued. From this we see the importance of building human bonds across religious, racial, and ethnic lines in times of relative social tranquil-ity. Otherwise, we will be in a poor position to try to establish those bonds in periods of social conflict and disruption.

Fourth, for us as Catholics, the witness of the righteous challenges our identity as a Church community. Dr. Helen Fein, writing in *Accounting for Genocide*, has argued that in the end many good people who faced difficult moral decisions under Nazi rule concluded that Jews could be regarded as "morally expendable." We, as Church, cannot allow that sort of calculation to persist any longer, whether for Jews or any other group of people. As Pope John Paul II has insisted in his writings, particularly in his encyclicals *Redemptor Hominis* and *Evangelium Vitae*, authentic belief in Christ demands a firm commitment to human dignity for all persons. The righteous continue to remind us of the need to place the struggle for human rights at the very center of Christian consciousness.

In closing, I wish to express my gratitude to the U.S. Holocaust Memorial Museum for honoring the Catholic righteous this afternoon. My pledge to you in the name of the Catholic bishops and other Catholics here assembled is that we as a Church will continue to combat anti-Semitism wherever, whenever, and in whatever form it may appear. May God's gift of shalom, peace, and health be with you all.

Washington, DC, April 15, 1997

9

We Remember

The Holy See's Statement on the Shoah

U.S. Conference of Catholic Bishops, Executive Session

I am grateful for this opportunity to offer to members of our conference some background on the document *We Remember: A Reflection on the Shoah*, issued on March 16 of this year by the Holy See's Commission for Religious Relations with the Jews.[1] First, I call your attention to the address given by Cardinal Edward I. Cassidy to the American Jewish Committee in Washington on May 15, 1998. This was shown on C-SPAN that evening and published in *Origins*.[2] It is an authentic and definitive commentary on and interpretation of *We Remember*, since Cardinal Cassidy issued the document and is the signatory. It clarifies key questions in the text.

The history of this document began in September 1987 while final preparations were being made for the visit of Pope John Paul II to our country. The audience granted by the Holy Father to Austrian Chancellor Kurt Waldheim deeply and understandably troubled Jewish leaders. At a meeting in Rome on

August 31, responding to their concerns, Cardinal Willebrands, who then headed the Commission for Religious Relations with the Jews, suggested that the commission publish a teaching document of the Church on the history of anti-Semitism with particular reference to our Church and the Shoah. The meeting produced other agreements mentioned in *We Remember*. A salient issue was the nature of the anti-Semitism that motivated the Shoah. As Jews and Catholics affirmed together in 1987, and as *We Remember* stresses, the anti-Semitism was rooted in a neopagan, anti-Christian ideology.

In 1990 in Prague, in 1992 in Baltimore, and in 1994 in Jerusalem, the International Catholic-Jewish Liaison Committee, which communicates between the Holy See's Commission for Religious Relations with Jews and the International Jewish Committee for Interreligious Consultations, met to exchange information and present papers on various phases of the Shoah. Finally, drafting was undertaken under the auspices of the commission. Here in the United States, we followed the process closely. Both Dr. Eugene Fisher and I had participated in the meetings leading to the preparation of the document and, through the years, we received and forwarded many inquiries from Jewish leaders regarding progress in development of the text.

We recognized that there would likely be a number of controversial questions relating to the document when it was published. For this reason I pointed out to the commission how useful it was for us in the United States to have copies of *Centesimus Annus, Veritatis Splendor*, and *Evangelii Nuntiandi* prior to publication. I requested of the commission that, if at all possible, we be given an advance copy of the Shoah document that we could share, under embargo, with some expert individuals in order to prepare them to make appropriate comments when it was published. Ideally, too, we would have circulated the document with some preliminary comment under embargo to the members of this conference.

On March 15, Dr. Fisher and I were in Jerusalem with a joint Catholic-Jewish pilgrimage involving five other bishops of this conference, seven rabbis, two priests, and a Jewish layperson. To our great surprise, we read in the *Jerusalem Post* that the document was to be published the next day. I telephoned the office of Cardinal Cassidy and eventually was able to speak with him. He explained to me that the office was closed and that it was not possible to send me a copy by fax. However, he did promise to send copies to us at the Rome airport the next day. That in fact occurred, at the very same time as the press conference was held to present the document to the world.

Later that day, Dr. Fisher and I spoke with the Catholic News Service and the *New York Times* and prepared a joint statement to be sent to all the dioceses. Cardinal O'Connor also issued a very helpful statement in New York. The next morning I received an apology from the Commission for Religious Relations with the Jews, explaining that they had received the final draft of the text only about noon on the Saturday before the Monday publication date. The Commission felt that they had no time to communicate the text to us and knew, indeed, that Dr. Fisher and I were in the Holy Land. They also knew that we were due in Rome for meetings with them on Tuesday.

The immediate reactions were various: Those Jewish leaders who have been close to us and sympathetic with us but not knowledgeable of details regarding particular issues were generally quite favorable in their reactions. Those who have been close to us and have become very familiar with various issues were positive in their reaction but critical of some aspects of the presentation in the text. Those who were not close to us through working relationships made very hostile statements, in great measure because they had unrealistic expectations about the document.

I want to reaffirm now what Dr. Fisher and I said in our statement at the time the document was issued. Over the years, this instruction on the Shoah will be extremely helpful both for internal catechesis in our Church and in our relationships with the Jewish people. A number of us remembered the initial reaction to *Nostra Aetate*, the fundamental document for the Church's relations with non-Christian religions. At first it was highly criticized, especially among Jewish leaders. And yet it has become the basis for an extraordinary change and deepening of spirit within our Church. The new document, like *Nostra Aetate*, is written in Catholic language and intended for use throughout the world, not just in those places where there are significant numbers of Jews or where the memories of the Holocaust burn so brightly. It is not fair to compare this document, which is intended for teaching a billion people around the world, with the documents issued by the individual bishops' conferences located in the lands in which the Holocaust claimed the greatest number of victims.

We Remember offers a basis for asserting the historic reality of the Shoah, something our Jewish friends find very helpful. It encourages our schools and religious education programs to undertake teaching about the Holocaust, and it urges further study and dialogue. As Cardinal Cassidy has pointed out, the Nazi persecution of the Jews utilized an "anti-Jewish prejudice imbedded in some Christian minds and hearts."[3]

The issuance of the document is particularly appropriate as we begin our preparations for the Great Jubilee in which interreligious considerations and dialogues are to have a part. I close by noting three issues that will be with us for a while.

First, whenever we speak of the Shoah, we should recall a point made clearly by Jewish and Catholic delegates together at the liaison committee in 1987: the Nazi Shoah, while directed against Jews with a view toward their total extermination, was also anti-Christian. The Nazi ideology drew on "the anti-Semitism of the 19th and 20th centuries based on racism and extreme forms of nationalism, theories contrary to the constant teaching of the Church on the unity of the human race and on the equal dignity of all races and peoples."[4] Especially in Poland many Catholics suffered, beginning in 1939, shortly after the Nazi invasion of their land. In some dioceses more than half of the priests were rounded up and executed within two months of the German invasion. As Dr. Stanislaus Krajewski has stated, "Most Holocaust survivors in the United States are Jewish, while most who live in Poland are Catholics. Each group has painful memories of those terrible days and each has nourished those memories apart from dialogue with the others." We must do anything we can to assist Jews to understand the suffering of others during that time and to help Catholics, especially in Poland, to see in context the Jewish memories of those horrific days.

Second, our culture has unfortunately been colored by the caricature of Pope Pius XII put forth by the German Protestant author Rolf Hochhuth in his play *The Deputy*, which portrays Pius as abstaining from any action. The historic record, as brought out by Kenneth Woodward's article in *Newsweek* and by other authors in other publications, shows that Pius did more than any other major leader at that time to help Jews escape extermination. Note also that the historical record has not been fully explored, so we have the commitment of the Holy See's commission to enter into joint research of published and, where there is clear indication of some unpublished relevant texts to be explored, other documents relating to that period.

Third, there is the issue of the canonization of Edith Stein, now known as Blessed Benedicta of the Cross, which is to take place on October 11, 1998. This is an issue of great sensitivity to our Jewish friends. I have found that when they are informed of the facts surrounding her death, they understand much more readily what the Church is doing in proposing her as a saint. As Pope John Paul II said when beatifying her, Edith Stein was martyred first because she was a Jew, but also because she was a Catholic. The Catholic bishops of Holland protested publicly the Nazi

roundup of the Jews in the spring of 1942. In retaliation, the
Nazis imprisoned Catholics of Jewish blood, including Edith
Stein, and these were sent by train to Auschwitz and Birkenau for
extermination.

Although born Jewish, Edith Stein abandoned the faith of
her parents when she was in her teens. A decade later, after having won her doctorate in philosophy and shown herself a brilliant
student, she embraced Catholicism and entered the Discalced
Carmelite monastery in Cologne, Germany. After *Kristallnacht*,
with its open Nazi hostility to the Jews, the Carmelites transferred her, for greater safety, to the monastery in Amsterdam.
Following the Nazi invasion of Holland, the evil that had been
feared in Germany became a reality in Holland. Since the beatification, our Jewish friends who have followed the situation
closely have been pleased to learn that Catholics have used her
life as a way of teaching about the reality of the Holocaust and
also as a witness to deeply spiritual values that promote reconciliation rather than enmity.

Finally, I sum up our present situation by echoing Cardinal
Edward Cassidy and asserting that *We Remember* marks the first
step in a new period of study, dialogue, and teaching—not the
end of the road.

Pittsburgh, June 26, 1998

10
Looking to the Future in Catholic-Jewish Relations

Pontifical North American College

It is always a joy to visit the Pontifical North American College and to speak in this auditorium, which I had the privilege of dedicating in 1997. I count it a blessing to share the platform with a dear friend and great scholar, Rabbi Jack Bemporad, who was the principal drafter of the Prague Declaration of 1990, from which Pope John Paul II has frequently quoted.

On March 16, 1998, the day on which *We Remember: A Reflection on the Shoah* was published, Dr. Eugene Fisher and I issued from Rome a first reflection on its impact. We saw it as a mandate for Catholic education on the Holocaust and as a resource for preparing for the Great Jubilee Year 2000. Pope John Paul II had already designated this year, 1999, as a time for special consideration of issues of interfaith dialogue and cooperation. The numerous programs around the United States in recent months have validated our prediction. This conference and the ceremonies that will follow are signs of commitment on the part of both Jews and Catholics to press forward in common efforts of discussion and collaboration.

Cardinal Cassidy's remarks later today will bring an authoritative word from the Holy See. Meanwhile, I wish to speak of several events that promise to impact our relationships on an international basis. Pope John Paul II has spoken of the Jubilee as an occasion for an examination of conscience on the part of the Church. Conferences relating to the Jubilee and dealing with the Inquisition and anti-Judaism have already been held in Rome. There surely will be other declarations by the pope in the context of two major events during the year 2000.

One of these events is already inscribed in the published Jubilee calendar: October 3 is dedicated to Christian-Jewish dialogue. The second event, I believe, will be a journey of the Holy Father to the Holy Land. Catholics and Jews share the hope for peace in the region. Like Jews, we Catholics pray "for the peace of Jerusalem," a prayer that will encourage the pope on his pilgrimage. The visit will provide him with an opportunity to continue to educate Catholics about the Holocaust in the context of the founding of the Jewish State, and on the place of the Law and the Prophets in our own theology. Media interest will be significant, helping relationships among Islam, Judaism, and Christianity. It will reinforce the desire for true theological dialogue, with parties meeting in mutual respect to discuss issues of faith close to their hearts.

The Christian minority in the Holy Land—Israel, Jerusalem, and the territories—has felt great pressure on it to emigrate. When our Jewish-Catholic pilgrimage visited there a year ago, we heard the same lament from Israeli Jews and Palestinian Muslims and Christians. All said that ways must be found to honor this minority and to stem or even reverse the tide of emigration. A Christian absence would be a tragedy for the land that all three great monotheistic traditions call holy.

Father John Pawlikowski of Chicago has reminded us on many occasions of the sensitive situation in Poland. Rabbi Jack Bemporad, Dr. Fisher, and I were part of a group of some twenty Jewish and six Catholic participants, including Father Pawlikowski, for a memorable visit to Poland in the summer of 1992. In Warsaw, at the invitation of Archbishop Henryk Muszyński, chair of the Polish Bishops' Committee for Dialogue with Judaism, we participated in one of its meetings. Dr. Stanislaus Krajewski, a Polish Jew who worked with the committee, pointed out that especially when the words are communicated through statements and press releases issued at a distance, unnecessary misunderstandings and conflicts can occur. A dramatic moment of our trip came when a Polish Catholic survivor of Birkenau joined us and met two Jewish survivors who were part of our party. Through their conversations, he discovered that a Catholic friend of his had made possible the woman's escape from the death camp.

The large cross and smaller crosses at Auschwitz are among the current symbols of memories at odds with each other, memories that cry out to heaven for healing. A month after our "traveling dialogue" visited Poland, I was back again, this time as part of a delegation of the officers of our U.S. Conference of Catholic Bishops. Two events from this trip stand out in my memory: The bishop who escorted us, an associate secretary of the Polish Bishops' Conference, told us that his father had been interned at Auschwitz and had somehow survived, but that he would never discuss what had transpired during his days there. His father would become quiet and stare at the wall, and sadness would envelop the conversation. The other event was a meeting of the officers of the Polish conference, led by Cardinal Josef Glemp, the president. I spoke in support of the proposal of Rabbi James Rudin of the American Jewish Committee that an exchange of seminary professors begin, with a Jewish professor from the United States to lecture in a Polish Catholic seminary and someone from Poland undertaking a similar mission at a Jewish seminary in the U.S. The bishops agreed and subsequently implemented the proposal.

But this is just the beginning of what needs to be done. Different tasks remain. As Archbishop Muszyński has reminded us, there are so few Jews in Poland that dialogue there is difficult. Catholics must engage in more detailed studies documenting the experiences of *Catholics* during the Nazi years. For example, it was news to many when Archbishop Muszyński reported about the Nazi invaders' direct attack on Catholic leaders within two months of the German invasion of Poland in September of 1939. In some dioceses, including his own, more than half the priests were rounded up and never seen again, the presumption in most cases being that they were executed and buried in remote wooded areas.

The biography of Cardinal Stefan Wyszyński (1901–81) recounts his wartime experiences, eluding the Nazis and narrowly escaping capture. At the direction of the bishop, he left the city where he was a seminary professor a very short time before the Gestapo arrested the entire seminary body in October 1939, shipping forty-six off to a concentration camp. Those who survived did not return until after the liberation of the camps at the end of the war.

Cardinal Wyszyński's biographer, Andrzej Micewski, attributes to Wyszyński this statement, published in a 1945 leaflet, regarding the Vatican radio broadcasts directed to Poland: "If sometimes news about Poland was scarce and tragic moments were passed over in silence, this was done only at the request of the Polish bishops who had discovered that the Germans took revenge on our prisoners for programs about their exploits in Poland."[1]

We are already familiar with concerns regarding the role of the Church throughout Europe during the Second World War and about the role of individual Catholics and other Christians, some of whom risked their lives as rescuers while others, sadly the majority, remained silent or sometimes even cooperated in the genocidal activities of the Nazi rulers. Here, another area for serious research and study suggests itself, beyond what is contemplated with respect to the Vatican archives. This involves other archival sources, the files of governments and of individuals and, while this may still be possible, the recollections of the living. Holocaust researchers have done a magnificent job working with

Jewish survivors and have produced significant insights into the lives of some of the rescuers. But much more needs to be done, especially in Poland, Italy, France, and the Balkan countries.

More study can and should be done about the political and moral settings of the day. An interesting example is the book, published two years ago in Milan, on the service of Archbishop Cesare Orsenigo, the papal nuncio in Berlin from 1930 to 1946. What emerges from his own notes at the time, his letters home, and his reports filed with the Holy See is the total control that was exercised by the Nazi apparatus over public life, the very little influence that he as the pope's representative had in his dealings with German officials, and the contempt with which the authorities, including Hitler, treated him and the Church for which he spoke.

Such studies will supplement and encourage the work of our teachers of religion, Catholic and Jewish. I suspect that the leadership of those gathered here today will help make possible, sooner than some may expect, the presence in all our Catholic schools—elementary and secondary, university and seminary level—programs on the Holocaust in all its painful complexity, fulfilling the Holy Father's approval of Holocaust studies in Catholic schools, which he expressed in his 1987 address to Jewish leaders in Miami, Florida.

We can take heart as well from Pope John Paul II's post-synodal exhortation *Ecclesia in America* on January 22 in Mexico City, which sets forth the synod's vision for America and relations between the Church and Jewish communities in the Western hemisphere:

> American society also includes Jewish communities, with which the Church has fostered increasing cooperation in recent years. The history of salvation makes clear our special relationship with the Jewish people. Jesus belongs to the Jewish people and he inaugurated

his Church within the Jewish nation. A great part of the Holy Scriptures, which we Christians read as the word of God, constitute a spiritual patrimony which we share with Jews. Consequently, any negative attitude in their regard must be avoided, since "in order to be a blessing for the world, Jews and Christians need first to be a blessing for each other."[2]

As we look to the future, we may also anticipate actions that speak louder than words by way of symbol in a world made one in the media. A papal visit to Jerusalem, Israel, and the lands under the Palestinian Authority may be complemented by other symbolic steps, such as a concert with an interfaith emphasis in Rome, recalling the enormous impact of the Holocaust concert of 1994. There may be more occasions like the one in Wroclaw, Poland, in 1997, when John Paul II used a Catholic Eucharistic Congress for an interfaith event at which he spoke on the need for dialogue and cooperation and then, with all Poland watching on live television, embraced the other participants. The three rabbis came last in line. When the pope embraced them, the more-than-10,000 people present, most of them Poles, thundered their applause. The pope's ancient title of *Pontifex Maximus*, the great bridge builder, seemed fully justified in that instant.

One hopes there will be more services like that in St. Louis in January, when in the presence of the pope, a rabbi read the scriptural lesson for the event, a reading from the prophet Isaiah; thus, the special ties between Church and Synagogue were made evident in a way that recalled the impact of the pope's 1986 visit to the Great Synagogue of Rome. This event has already made a significant positive impression on those engaged in the dialogue. Today's dedication of the Yom Hashoah Menorah represents another major step in implementing Pope John Paul II's vision of our major faith communities moving together to make sure that the lessons of the Holocaust are not forgotten. These lessons are all the more timely in the light of the events of recent years in Cambodia, the Sudan, and now Kosovo.

As we look forward now to the dedication of the menorah, I express my gratitude to Gunther Lawrence for organizing this significant event. The menorah has artistic power and beauty. It will be seen by many, including the one hundred or so seminarians currently studying for the priesthood in dioceses throughout the United States.

In his introduction to *We Remember*, Pope John Paul II stressed how, in approaching the Great Jubilee, the Church "encourages her sons and daughters to purify their hearts through repentance of past errors and infidelities." He expressed hope that this may "enable memory to play its necessary part in the process of shaping a future in which the unspeakable iniquity of the *Shoah* will never again be possible."[3]

The menorah we dedicate this afternoon will help to nourish reflection. It will no doubt be more powerful than any word spoken today. Sadly, in the past, words have often failed to produce a change of heart. Several years ago I contributed an article to a festschrift honoring Rabbi Alexander Schindler in which I presented quotations from public statements of the Catholic bishops of the United States. The American bishops, who met in Washington, DC, in November of 1938, just after *Kristallnacht*, utilized the entire period of a national radio broadcast to issue a series of denunciations of what one called "a shameless orgy of ruthless oppression, even extinction, willed by the mad lust for power...upon a helpless, already shackled people."[4] Gershon Greenberg, assessing the role of American Catholics during the Holocaust, cites a number of public and private interventions of members of the Catholic hierarchy to denounce Hitler and "safeguard the rights of Jewish victims." Greenberg speaks of the interventions with the United States and other governments made by the apostolic delegate of the Holy See to the United States, and by Archbishop Giovanni Cicognani, who represented Pope Pius XII in our country.[5]

In 1942, encouraged by Archbishop Cicognani, the American bishops made a major statement about the Jewish plight. Among them were Cardinal Dennis Dougherty of Philadelphia and cardinals-to-be Spellman of New York, Stritch of Chicago, and Mooney of Detroit. (In 1946, they met in Philadelphia again, this time to select Bishop Martin J. O'Connor to be rector of this college.)

Please God that our common resolve today, echoed in our educational work and our efforts at dialogue in both our faith communities, will make such words as they spoke in 1942 forever unnecessary in the future.

Washington, DC, April 13, 1999

11
National Workshop on Christian-Jewish Relations

Keynote Address

With gratitude I return to this workshop, which provides to so many in the field of Christian-Jewish relations an opportunity to be refreshed by what is new in the world of scholarship and refreshed by the old and the new in friendships celebrated around common interests. There is a quality about this gathering that reminds me of a story told by John Westerhoff. A few years ago, he was conducting a series of conferences on the Scriptures in Northern Ireland and found that, after several days, the adult participants, Protestant and Catholic, were not reconciling but rather were continuing to talk at each other, words passing in the air without being heard. While the adults sat in a circle of chairs, youngsters played on the floor. One day a priest decided to sit, not in a chair with the adults, but on the floor with the children, next to a little Protestant girl. On that day, Westerhoff lectured on how Jesus healed the woman who touched his garment. The little girl said to the priest next to her, "My father wouldn't like it if I touched you." She touched him and then said, "Nothing has happened." The priest answered, "Everything has happened. Neither of us will ever see the world again in the same way." From that moment, the flavor of the meeting changed and all began to listen as well as to speak—surely part of an emerging pattern that prepared the way for the Good Friday Accord that opened up the hopes for peace.

We are here today because, whether years ago or recently, we ourselves had an opportunity to be touched by a person or by an event, and, like the Irish in the story, began to open our minds and hearts to new horizons.

This workshop meets on the vigil of what Christians prepare to celebrate as the great Jubilee Year 2000. Several years ago in the course of a regular meeting of the ongoing consultation between the USCCB and the National Council of Synagogues, we Catholics asked our partners in dialogue what we might share together on the occasion of the Jubilee. They were silent at first. The coming of Jesus did not compute as an event for the Jewish community.

But our discussion continued, and they recognized that we were going to mark the event and would value their counsel. Dr. Eugene Fisher observed that we could well note the coming two-thousandth anniversary of Christian-Jewish relations! We did, in fact, issue a joint statement on the millennium expressing our common concerns and hopes as religious leaders. As I scan the scene today, and as a pastor speaking from a Roman Catholic perspective, I too note some concerns, concerns matched by hopes that fair-minded people are more interested in peace than war, and in mutual understanding than continued bickering and bitterness.

In terms of printer's ink, the issue of Pope Pius XII currently receives the most attention. Today I make two points: Critics should see Pius XII in a context true to the times in which he lived. And we should all see how this controversy harks back to a sad period in our American history.

It is important to judge Pope Pius XII in the context of his own experience of the role, power, and influence of the papacy. A brief historical review will remind us of the kind of papacy that he inherited. As for the papacy's authority within the Church, it certainly could not be greater than it was in his day. However, in terms of the papacy's influence in secular affairs, Pius XII began his pontificate at the end of a troubled century and a half, during which the papacy had reached a low point, a nadir, in terms of political power.

In the wake of the French Revolution, two popes were taken as prisoners into exile by the French—Pius VI and Pius VII. Napoleon kept Pius VII in seclusion near Paris for almost two years and browbeat him into signing a draft concordat that gave away the liberty of the Church, an act that the pope quickly repented. After Napoleon's fall, the papacy recovered most of its temporal possessions that, however, now became almost a protectorate of the Austrian empire. The papacy of that era cherished temporal power precisely because this assured freedom from domination by secular powers. After the revolutionary year of 1848, the political trends in European governments were generally unfavorable to the temporal power of the papacy and often to the claims of religion within society. As the Italian struggle for independence and unification progressed, the papal states by 1860 fell almost entirely under the dominion of the new Kingdom of Italy, and Rome alone was left for the pope, now as a protectorate of the French Empire. The final blow came ten years later, when the Kingdom of Italy seized Rome after French troops withdrew to fight the Franco-Prussian war.

Pius IX and his successors rejected the arrangement for the papacy that had been unilaterally adopted by the Kingdom of Italy, since it left the pope subject to Italian domestic politics. The pope became the "prisoner of the Vatican." Initially, Catholics were forbidden by the pope to participate in the political life of the Kingdom of Italy. Faithful Catholics were divided about the wisdom of the ban on political activity that left them with little influence in their own country. "The Roman Question" became a thorn in the side of the Italian government.

Despite the loss of temporal power, the papacy saw an increase in its moral prestige. However, that did not prevent Bismarck from making war on the Catholic subjects during his *Kulturkampf* of the new German Reich of the 1870s. Nor did it prevent an anti-clerical mob in 1878 from trying to throw the coffin of the newly deceased Pius IX into the Tiber on its way to its final resting place. And neither did it stop anti-religious legislation around the turn of the century during the reigns of Leo XIII and Pius X, legislation enacted in France and Italy by governments often dominated by radically anti-clerical forces. To make matters more difficult, faithful Catholics in countries with religiously hostile governments were sometimes divided among themselves about how to deal with matters. In the United States, Catholic immigrants faced discrimination and hostility, often fueled by caricatures of the papacy and attacks upon it. Later from the same nativist circles came similar discrimination against the Jews, with the *Protocols of the Elders of Zion* serving a role similar to the anti-papal screeds.

Things did not improve quickly in Italy or elsewhere. Benedict XV was pope during World War I. He was a skilled diplomat who considerably increased the number of nations with which the Holy See had diplomatic relations. Throughout the war, the Vatican's relief efforts were successful and much valued. However, Benedict also proposed principles for a just peace. The reactions to his efforts by governments and faithful Catholics were often unfavorable. Each side criticized him as being in favor of their foes. Even a prayer for peace that he wrote was initially not permitted to be prayed publicly in France. He worked hard to reserve Italian neutrality, but Italy eventually entered the war in 1915. The Italian government obtained the exclusion of the Holy See from an active role in the Treaty of Versailles, probably for fear that the pope's representatives would bring up the "Roman Question."

The "Roman Question" was settled only in 1929 with the Lateran Treaty, which was negotiated between Pius XI and

Mussolini. However, *Il Duce* acted not out of concern for the Church but out of desire to gain the support of Catholics. The same can be said of the Concordat of 1933 that the Third Reich concluded with the Holy See. In the case of both nations, Pius XI eventually was forced to denounce the not-unexpected violations of the treaties.

When considering the willingness of Pius XI to sign concordats with Fascist Italy and Nazi Germany, we must recall how often the Holy See, in the late nineteenth and early twentieth centuries, had to deal with governments hostile to religion in general or Catholicism in particular. Putting the Holy See's diplomatic house in order through a series of concordats—such as those with Spain and Hungary—was the policy of Pope Pius XI. What is more interesting is how clearly he recognized the invidiousness of the relatively new approach of totalitarianism, with its complete subordination of the individual to the state. This approach he condemned.

These, then, were the times into which Pope Pius XII was dropped. Born Eugenio Pacelli in 1876 in Rome, the son of a lawyer who worked for the Holy See, he grew up with the image of a papacy whose secular power had been extinguished in its own domain. Under Pius XI, Pacelli—as cardinal and Vatican secretary of state—contributed to restoring the prestige of the papacy in secular matters, so that the papacy he himself inherited was gradually coming back from the diplomatic isolation it suffered in the last quarter of the nineteenth century. Even so, he remembered that the secular powers had largely scorned Benedict XV's efforts for peace in World War I, and Benedict's experience undoubtedly influenced him twenty-five years later.

Thus, when Pacelli was elected pope in 1939 and took the name Pius XII, he knew the limits of papal influence with secular governments. He was convinced that patient diplomacy was needed if the papacy were to have any chance of influencing hostile secular power. Stalin, an almost exact contemporary of Pius

XII, had good reason to ask, disdainfully, "How many divisions has the pope?"

The facts of the Holocaust demonstrate that the world community, including the Church, failed the Jews of Nazi Germany and of the nations it controlled. What grieves many Catholics—and angers others—is the singular concentration on the supposed default of Pius XII. National leaders also have an obligation to be moral leaders, but the leaders of the nations at war with Hitler did not speak out on behalf of those being slaughtered. Few have been more eloquent than Roosevelt and especially Churchill, and yet neither martialed the English language in defense of the Jews of Germany. Large international organizations, including humanitarian ones, did not seek to influence the behavior of Nazi Germany by exposing its horrors to the world. As a result, Catholics ask whether Pius XII has been used as a scapegoat to avoid dealing with all this silence. Catholics in the United States familiar with the anti-papal rhetoric of the last century and up to the Kennedy election in the twentieth century see a sad echo of another era in the allegations about Pope Pius XII. I wish to make it clear that I am not imputing guilty motives to these other public figures. Nazi Germany was a criminal state. Hitler and those around him came to power through coercing their opponents. They could not be expected to behave in the predictable manner that is necessary for successful diplomacy.

We Catholics find the singling out of Pius XII particularly troubling because he at least let the world know of his concern. In his 1942 Christmas message, he spoke of the "hundreds of thousands who, through no fault of their own, and solely because of their nation or race, have been condemned to death or progressive extinction." Contemporary reports show that his words were clearly understood in Nazi Germany, where the pope was described as "virtually accusing the German people of injustice toward the Jews, and mak[ing] himself the mouthpiece of Jewish war criminals."[1] He spoke in similar fashion to his Curia in June

1943, adding that "every word from us in this regard to the competent authorities" needed to be weighed carefully "in the very interest of those who suffer so as not to make their position even more difficult and more intolerable than previously, even though inadvertently and unwillingly."

Pope Pius XII was not going to make the lives of others the price of his own reputation for prophetic denunciation. Dismissal of the papal language as "evasive" is not an argument but actually a refusal to consider the evidence in the context of the diplomatic language the Holy See habitually used at the time. The nuncios who worked on behalf of the Jews—doing things outside of usual diplomatic activities and even skirting Church law— were in a good position to know and be influenced by the pope's attitudes. They did not feel hampered either by a supposed sympathetic attitude to Nazi Germany or by an unsympathetic attitude to helping the Jewish victims of Nazism.

Since the play *The Deputy*, many Catholics see Pius XII as the target of something akin to propaganda's "big lie" technique. Accusing a pope of not doing enough would hardly bring a play to Broadway. Accuse him of dereliction of duty out of bigotry or other unsavory motives and you have a full house. It also leaves the pope's defenders with the nearly impossible chore of proving a negative: "No, Pius XII is not the villain of the piece."

The historical record clearly does not support these distortions. Nothing in it comes remotely close to showing that Pius XII was a supporter of Hitler or that he was unconcerned about the treatment of Jews. So Catholics ask themselves why an argument over a hypothetical has become such an issue between Catholics and Jews today. Those interested in history delight in "what if" discussions: "What if Pius XII had made the kind of statement that he is criticized for not making, and it had brought on a murderous assault by the Nazis? Would we today be discussing his folly and not his silence?" But these discussions are fruitless. They can have no conclusion because there is no alternative history. To condemn a pope on such hypothetical grounds is perhaps to be influenced by factors other than the purely historical. For instance, no one can read John Cornwell's book *Hitler's Pope* without noticing that he has a problem with the role of the papacy in the Church today. It would be hard not to speculate how his views on the latter affect his historical judgment of Pius XII.

An excellent summary of the mass of often-conflicting advice the pope received can be found in Father Pierre Blet's *Pius XII and the Second World War* (Mahwah, NJ: Paulist Press, 1999). The reader will also find there the pope's various obligations that were not easily balanced one with another, and the simple difficulty of getting and giving information in a world at war. Pius's approval of and involvement with the German army's plot against Hitler may well indicate that he knew in his heart what those at war with Nazi Germany concluded: Hitler could not be persuaded, only defeated.

There are other significant factors that must be considered in any judgment of Pius XII. There is the faith perspective of the informed Catholic. Those familiar with the inner history of our Church in this century know that it was precisely Pope Pius XII who, by his encyclicals on biblical studies (*Divino Afflante Spiritu*, 1943), on their application to ecclesiology (*Mystici Corporis*, 1943), and on the liturgy (*Mediator Dei*, 1947), prepared the way for the epochal debates and decisions of the Second Vatican Council. His vision and commitment to these issues brought to the fore people like Cardinal Augustin Bea, one of his closest collaborators, who later became, under Pope John XXIII, the principal proponent and architect for ecumenical, Catholic-Jewish, and interfaith dialogue and understanding—contributing heavily to *Nostra Aetate*.

The Christmas messages of Pope Pius XII also presented principles for the development of democracies that helped inspire political parties of Christian orientation in Italy, France, and

Germany during the postwar era. For many years I have been repeating words I heard from Rabbi Mordecai Waxman: "If you really love me, you would know what causes me pain." Our Jewish partners in dialogue are rightly pained by attempts to misrepresent the reality of the Holocaust or to miscast the role of the State of Israel. Likewise, many Catholics, aware of the role of Pius XII in the broader context of history, are hurt by attacks reminiscent of the caricatures of nativists of another period in American history.

I have great confidence that the fairness of the Jewish people will assert itself on behalf of a balanced memory of Pius XII. Knowing the responsibility their people so often have had to bear for problems they did not cause, I am convinced that the many Jewish friends I have come to know well and respect deeply would not wish that same fate for a pope whose wartime record is so demonstrably superior to the picture presented by those who, from whatever motive, chose to malign him.

Several years ago I contributed an article to a festschrift honoring Rabbi Alexander Schindler. In it, I presented quotations from public statements of the Holy See and Catholic bishops of the United States. Pius XI's 1937 encyclical *Mit brennender Sorge* condemned the teaching of Nazism, especially its "racialism." It had a galvanizing effect on the American Catholic community. Cardinal Pacelli, later Pope Pius XII, was the principal drafter of the document.

The American bishops, meeting in Washington in November of 1938, just after *Kristallnacht,* used the entire period of their annual national radio broadcast to issue a series of denunciations of what one called "a shameless orgy of ruthless oppression, even extinction, willed by the mad lust for power." Archbishop Cicognani, who represented Pope Pius XII to the Catholics of our country during the war years, encouraged the American bishops during World War II to make a major statement about the Jewish plight. Issued on November 14, 1942, it contained the following strong appeal:

> Since the murderous assault on Poland, utterly devoid of every semblance of humanity, there has been a premeditated and systematic extermination of the people of the nation. The same satanic technique is being applied to many other peoples. We feel a deep sense of revulsion against the cruel indignities heaped upon the Jews in conquered countries and upon defenseless peoples not of our faith. We join with our brother bishops in subjugated France: "Deeply moved by the mass arrests and maltreatment of Jews, we cannot stifle the cry of our conscience. In the name of humanity and Christian principles our voice is raised in favor of imprescriptible rights of human nature." We raise our voice in protest against despotic tyrants who have lost all sense of humanity by condemning thousands of innocent persons to death in subjugated countries as acts of reprisal, by placing other thousands of innocent victims in concentration camps, and by permitting unnumbered persons to die of starvation.[2]

Please God that our common resolve today, echoed in our educational work and our efforts at dialogue in both our faith communities, will make such words as they spoke in 1942 forever unnecessary in the future.

Houston, October 24, 1999

12
National Jewish Council for Public Affairs

Thank you, Mr. Mel Shralow, for your gracious words of introduction. I shall tell Rabbi Joel Zaiman of your kindness and that of Larry Rudin in inviting me. Joel and Larry were part of a "traveling dialogue" to Israel and Rome two years ago. We shared visits to each other's holy places, briefings from local authorities, and growth in mutual understanding. We Catholics attended synagogue services on the Sabbath and the Feast of Purim. At Capernaum in Galilee, an especially poignant moment came when we met on the site of a second-century synagogue. Dr. Eugene Fisher recalled that it was there, nearly two millennia earlier, that Jesus had taught in the synagogue of his day. Our coming meant that successors of the apostles were in peaceful dialogue with successors of the scribes and Pharisees who were interlocutors with Jesus.

That region always is much in the news. I wish to say a word now about recent developments in the light of our own local, Maryland history. Our state had its roots in the only colony from England under Catholic leadership. The colonists came in 1634 with the understanding that, under the governorship of the Calvert family, Catholics and others could freely practice their religious faith according to the dictates of the individual conscience. In the Acts of Toleration of 1639 and 1649, we have the first instance in the English-speaking world of the beginning of protected religious freedom as we know it. It was not perfect, because it embraced only the people then in the colony, who were Christians. But it did honor the faith of the Protestants who comprised a significant percentage of the early settlers. In the aftermath of the Glorious Revolution (1688), the English crown replaced the Calverts and sent royal governors to enforce in Maryland the English penal laws against Catholics. All the Catholic churches in the colony were razed to the ground, and Mass could not be celebrated publicly. Priests could not hold property and often were arrested for little cause. The Catholic laity could not hold public office or vote in elections, and they paid double taxes. Thus, when the American Revolution came along, Catholic leadership in Maryland gave strong support to the movement. Father John Carroll, who was to become the first bishop in our country, and his cousin Charles Carroll of Carrollton, joined Benjamin Franklin and Samuel Chase as emissaries of the Continental Congress to Canada. They tried in vain to persuade the predominantly Catholic Province of Quebec to join in the quest for independence from England.

Charles Carroll signed the Declaration of Independence with a large, boldly written signature to assert as strongly as possible his commitment to the cause. Back in Maryland Carroll, educated as an attorney in England but forbidden to practice law because of his faith, was invited to draft the state constitution of Maryland. He wrote what stands to this day as perhaps the most forceful assertion of religious freedom in any legal document anywhere. And he ardently promoted the adoption of the First Amendment of the U.S. Constitution.

Although Catholics, like the Jewish immigrants after them, continued to suffer many hindrances and encounter much prejudice, the protection afforded by the constitution helped our people, as it helped yours, to flourish religiously in ways unique in the world. When my distinguished predecessor Cardinal James Gibbons went to Rome in 1887 to receive the cardinal's red hat, he spoke with pride of the liberty all Americans enjoyed in the practice of religious faith and in the pursuit of individual destinies. "There are indeed grave social problems which are engaging the earnest attention of the citizens of the United States. But I have no doubt that, with God's blessings, these problems will be solved without violence, or revolution, or injury to individual rights."[1]

Gibbons' position, and that of our leadership in the United States, was not always welcome in some Catholic circles in Europe. When the Second Vatican Council came in the early 1960s, the bishops of the United States were principal movers in promoting the Council's Declaration on Religious Liberty. Cardinal Lawrence Shehan of Baltimore and others from the States supported the vision of Father John Courtney Murray, SJ, who taught at the Jesuit seminary in Woodstock, Maryland. On December 7, 1965, the Council voted its approval of the declaration, 2,308 to 70. Subsequently, agreements were reached with a number of countries where Catholics made up the majority of citizens, as in Spain and Latin America, to assure freedom of all faith groups to practice their faith, where there had been restrictions before.

Against this background, I turn to questions raised last week by the agreement between the Holy See and the PLO. An official commentary published the other day in *L'Osservatore Romano* recalls an address of Pope John Paul II in 1993 calling for true religious freedom throughout the Middle East and appealing to the teaching of our Second Vatican Council. He called on the Christian communities there to realize that

> although they live in a region in which there are undertakings inspired by different religious beliefs,...they should recognize that the dignity of the human person is unique, indivisible, unrepeatable and as such to be respected and guaranteed....[Thus,] belonging to one

religion can never be a reason for discrimination; nor should anyone be viewed simply as a guest in his or her own country.

The pope went on to point out that international law was now calling on governments to modify internal laws to reflect principles of religious and other freedoms. This looked toward the "assurance of parity of treatment for every person, independently of his or her ethnic, language, cultural and religious background." The agreement last week between the Holy See and the PLO has attracted a great deal of attention. From a Catholic perspective let me shed a little light.

In a practical summary of the policy of the Holy See for the region, Archbishop Jean-Louis Tauran said at a meeting in Washington last March that he understood the need for a country like Israel to "live within clearly defined borders without having to be in a constant state of alert." When the bishops of the United States undertook the writing of the pastoral message "Toward Peace in the Middle East," the Israeli government provided us with an unforgettable helicopter tour of the land. This tour enabled us to see vividly and to report clearly what we had heard so often about the small and vulnerable size and shape of the State of Israel.

For two years the Holy See has been trying to provide, for Church institutions in territories under Palestinian control, the same legal protection that they have in Israeli territory. This protection came in virtue of the Fundamental Agreement between Israel and the Holy See in December 1993 with a subsequent exchange of ambassadors in 1994, and of the documents implementing the accord. As the Holy See said in the clarifying statement issued immediately after the initial reaction of the government of Israel, there is no attempt in the accord to "enter into questions of territoriality or sovereignty" in Jerusalem or anywhere in the region. The Holy See has repeatedly said, as we

American bishops also declared in our statement, that these are questions to be resolved by the parties to the negotiations, the Israelis and the Palestinians.

Indeed, it was to protect the principle that sovereignty can only be resolved by the parties who live there that the document restated the Holy See's traditional rejection of any unilateral claim to the city by any one party. The Jordanian claim to Jerusalem thus was rejected in 1948 in a document entitled *In Multiplicibus Curis* (In the Face of Multiple Preoccupations). Israel's 1967 Basic Law was likewise rejected as "unilateral" and invalid under international law by the Holy See in 1968. Now, the Holy See has succeeded in getting the PLO to reject its own unilateral claim to the city by means of this agreement. In the preamble, the PLO has also finally acknowledged, in an instrument recognized as binding under international law, the application of the principle of full religious liberty and freedom of conscience to its own society—the first Arab country to do so. This represents a very real breakthrough toward democracy in the Middle East. I can only pray that the idea will spread to other Arab countries such as Saudi Arabia.

So far, I believe, the Israeli government can have no quarrel with the Holy See's agreement with the PLO. Indeed, it should find much to be grateful for in the long run. Where there may be need for further discussion and clarification between Israel and the Holy See is in this question: What are the practical implications of the inclusion of the long-standing position of the Holy See that there be an "international statute" to "guarantee" the five principles listed in the agreement's preamble? The five principles themselves, of course, are not the problem. They have all been affirmed already by successive governments of Israel. They include protection of access to holy places and protection of the civil and religious liberties of all citizens of Jerusalem, whether Jewish, Christian, or Muslim, and continued respect for the status quo.

This is not a matter of the Holy See moving toward the position of the PLO, but of the PLO joining in an affirmation of long-standing principles put forth by the Holy See and already affirmed by the State of Israel. Here it is well to keep in mind that already in 1968 the Holy See ceased pushing for the UN's idea of "internationalization," that is, an "international status" for Jerusalem, guaranteeing its citizens basic religious rights. The latter, it is affirmed, can be worked out in such a way as to avoid unduly threatening the sovereignty of Israel, and would have to be so worked out or Israel would not sign on.

Here we arrive at what I see as the real nub of Israel's question about the preamble. How would such an international mechanism be worked out in practice? Could citizens of Jerusalem take the governments of Israel and/or a possible Palestinian entity to the World Court? And how would the court's decision be enforced? To my mind these are real, practical issues that the sovereign State of Israel can quite legitimately both raise directly with the Holy See now for clarification, and keep in mind later during its negotiations with the PLO. In the meantime, I believe that it is to everyone's long-range benefit that the Holy See has managed to raise these issues in a legitimate way with one of the parties involved in the peace process. We should all agree that the religious dimension of the city, especially the Old City, is not peripheral to a resolution of the Jerusalem question, but central to it.

The interreligious dimension of Jerusalem presents a series of issues that cannot properly be subsumed under other categories, whether cultural or educational, although it is clearly related to both. In the religious sensitivities of 2 billion Christians and certainly in the minds and hearts of 15 million Jews around the world, Jerusalem is not just an "earthly" reality but in some very real way a sacred, or "heavenly," reality. Why else would the mostly secular Jewish leaders who created and sustained the Jewish people's modern liberation movement have called their movement after a most religious understanding of Jerusalem—Holy Zion?

Every day I pray publicly for the peace of Jerusalem and that region. Many of you, I know, have the same prayer on your lips. Many people in our Church throughout the United States have this concern in our hearts and in our prayers. We are not simply echoing an ancient prayer of the psalmist but are expressing a very real need for our world today, if truly we are to come to peace. Let us continue to pray that the leaders of the region may see that their peoples will be truly blessed when those who lead them have the political and moral courage to make decisions that contribute to a peace that is based on justice, that offers security to Israel, and that gives the Palestinian people, at long last, a recognition of dignity and of peoplehood and a land they can call their own.

The events of the Holocaust years as they relate to Pope Pius XII and the Holy See are now being appropriately studied by a joint committee of serious scholars, coordinated on the Catholic side by our own Dr. Eugene Fisher. These scholars are examining the twelve published volumes of the Vatican archives that relate in most thorough detail to the years of Nazi domination in Europe. It is clear to me that such studies could be expanded to the archives of other nations in order to see in greater relief the possibilities and the challenges faced by the pope and by many others in that difficult time.

With respect to the Holy Land—Israel, Jerusalem, and the territories—we must note that this region has seen great pressures on the Christian minority to emigrate. When our interfaith pilgrimage visited there in March two years ago, we heard the same lament from Israeli Jews and from Palestinian Muslims and Christians. All said that ways must be found to honor this minority and to stem and even reverse the tide of emigration. A Christian absence would be a tragedy for the land that the three Abrahamic religions call holy.

Baltimore, February 28, 2000

13
Jay Phillips Center for Jewish-Christian Learning

On September 3, 2000, Pope John Paul II raised to the level of "blessed"—which is a step on the way to sainthood—Pope John XXIII, an act warmly welcomed and praised in the Jewish community. In the same ceremony, he officially bestowed on Pope Pius IX the same title of blessed. News accounts of the beatification of Pius IX have caused understandable difficulty among our Jewish friends. Let me say a word or two to put this in the context of our ongoing relationship.

As Pope John Paul II pointed out in his homily at the beatification Mass, John XXIII, beloved of us all, had an immense personal devotion to the memory of Pius IX. He wrote that he himself dreamed of being the instrument of God in the canonization of Pius IX. Why could he say this? The answer, I believe, lies in the nature of society 150 years ago and also in the personality of Blessed Pius IX. It was a period of extraordinary anti-Catholic and anti-religious sentiment, especially among governing powers in Europe and the United States. This was the period in which nativist mobs burned convents and churches in Boston, Philadelphia, and Baltimore, and threatened New York City with the most explosive of anti-Catholic riots. A frequent target of the nativists was the "popery" of Catholics. It is a period that many Americans, including many Catholics, have largely forgotten today. When Blessed Pius IX denounced "progress," he was speaking about the definition of "progress" given by anti-religious governments in Europe, which meant the elimination of the faith aspect from the lives of people.

Pope Pius IX rose above the constant negativity of the times to maintain personal equilibrium and to encourage good works. Some critics may accuse him of having been a pope-king—authoritarian and brutal. The historical record indicates otherwise, however. For instance, taxes paid to the Papal States at that time were half of what was paid in France to the authorities and a quarter of what was paid in England. Blessed Pius IX is accused of being opposed to progress. Yet, at a time when traveling by train was the privilege of a few, the pope had 250 miles of railroad tracks built in the state to serve the needs of ordinary people. He undertook great public works, such as the draining of the muddy terrains of Ostia and Ferrara. He improved and promoted agriculture, enlarged the principal ports on the Adriatic Sea, promoted gas illumination beginning in 1847, and promoted archaeological excavations and restoration works. Under his government, Rome had one hospital for every 9,000 inhabitants, while London had one for every 40,000. Rome had a charitable institute for every 2,700 inhabitants while London had one for every 7,000. Between 1850 and 1870, Pius IX promoted kindergartens, dormitories for the homeless, ovens that sold inexpensive bread for the indigent, public housing, and free medical centers for the poor.

What he did wrong, by our standards today and by the standards of many in his own day, was to support the Catholic upbringing of a young boy born of Jewish parents, who had been secretly baptized by his Catholic nurse when she thought him to be in danger of death. This is something that could not happen today. That it did happen then, as Peter Steinfels has sagely noted in the *New York Times*, has its parallel in the case of Elian Gonzalez. We remember how little Elian from Cuba represented a symbol whose significance was read in very diverse directions by two groups of people, both of whom were very ardent in their beliefs and equal in their good faith. So, Steinfels pointed out, Blessed Pius IX acted in accord with his conscience as shaped in the times in which he lived. As I said, what he did then would not be done today.

In 1987, a rabbi friend of mine told me about the action of a Polish priest in the days not long after the Second World War. A Catholic couple brought a child to him to be baptized. He asked why the child had not been baptized before. Their response was that the child was not theirs but had been born of another set of parents. The priest asked the religion of those parents. They responded, "Jewish." Then, he said, he could not baptize the child. His birth-parents' implied wish had to be respected. That Jewish child has grown to adulthood and now lives in our country. The story is a true one. The priest, as many of you already know, was Father Karol Wojtyla, now Pope John Paul II. One of the chief rabbis of Israel repeated the story to me and said that the pope, in response to a question, said the gentleman is still alive and now lives in Brooklyn.

There is also the story of Edith Stein, who received a great deal of attention in October 1999 when Pope John Paul II canonized her as St. Benedicta of the Cross. Her story illustrates the complexity and the horror of the Shoah. Edith Stein came from Breslau, in Silesia, then in Germany, and now known as Wroclaw in Poland. She grew up in a Jewish family, and by the time she was fifteen, she had lost all religious faith. She was a brilliant student and achieved a doctorate in philosophy and a prominent teaching position in a German university. When she was about twenty-five, she read the life of St. Teresa of Avila, who founded the reform of the Carmelite nuns in sixteenth-century Spain. Deeply impressed by the spiritual insights of Teresa, Edith began a pilgrimage of the heart that led her to become a Catholic and then a cloistered Carmelite nun.

In the latter part of the 1930s in Germany, the situation for Jews became such that the religious community of Sister Benedicta transferred her to a monastery in Holland. The Nazis invaded Holland and carried out the terrible roundup of the Jews in the spring of 1942. Christian leaders protested the roundup and were told by the Germans that if they made their protest public, their own people with Jewish blood would be subject to similar treatment. The Catholic bishops did in fact raise their voices publicly to protest what the Nazis were doing to the Jewish people of Holland. In consequence, the Nazis retaliated and Catholics of Jewish blood, including Sister Benedicta, were taken prisoner and sentenced to Auschwitz. One of the most touching stories I have read is the detailed account that has been pieced together of her trip from Holland to Southern Germany and Poland, and then to Auschwitz, documented day by day from the contacts she had with people in railroad stations on the way. In August 1942, Edith Stein was gassed with thousands of others at Auschwitz.

Edith Stein stands as a remarkable witness to the intensity and reality of the Shoah. As I have pointed out in an official statement and in many settings, her canonization serves to remind Catholics of the reality of the Holocaust, as well as the reality of human holiness and dedication to God and to God's ways in a world of confusion and contradiction. It may well be that history will show that Stein, Sister Benedicta of the Cross, was one of the most insightful spiritual writers of the century we are now closing.

My assigned and blessed task in promoting positive relationships and deeper understanding between the Catholic Church and the Jewish people in the United States has been made so much easier by the personal commitment and example of Pope John Paul II in the work of reconciliation. It strikes me that it would be useful this evening to reflect on the pope's visit to the Middle East in March of last year. What was a personal spiritual pilgrimage for the Holy Father also had meaning for many others.

The pope helped Catholics, and Christians generally, to see through his eyes places familiar from frequently recounted Bible stories. On his first day in Jordan, he recalled how Moses looked over to the Promised Land from Mount Nebo. The next day the pope referred to the nearby hometown of Isaiah the prophet and to what the cousin of Jesus, John the Baptist, had done in the land beyond the Jordan River. He greeted Orthodox and Protestant Christians, encouraging them in the role all Christians must continue to play in the birthplace of our faith.

When Pope John Paul II crossed over into Israel, his words and actions had meaning also for Jews and Muslims, for whom the region is also the Holy Land. I arrived in Jerusalem the Friday before the pope would on the following Tuesday evening. This was my eighth visit to the city, and I had never seen spirits higher. The flags of Israel and the Holy See fluttered along the main streets, and conversation everywhere turned on the coming visit.

From the outset of his preparations for this Year of Jubilee, Pope John Paul II drew inspiration from the Book of Leviticus and the prescriptions for the observation for the ancient jubilee. It was to be a time of forgiveness, with debts pardoned and burdens lifted. He undertook his pilgrimage in the penitential season of Lent, when the official prayers of the Catholic Church call our people to attitudes of repentance. Before he left Rome, he led a service in which he prayed for God's pardon for sins committed by Christian believers through the centuries, including the use of violence in the cause of religion. The pope thus showed how seriously the Catholic Church had proceeded in internalizing the teaching on religious freedom of the Second Vatican Council.

What Pope John Paul II taught Catholics while in Israel, besides reminding us of key events in the life and work of Jesus, helped us to deepen our understanding of the Holocaust. Since his first visit as pope to Poland in 1979, which included time at the death camp at Auschwitz-Birkenau, he pointed out to Catholic audiences the uniquely genocidal horror of the Holocaust for Jews. At Yad Vashem, standing in the somber memorial chamber, he dramatized this sad truth for Catholics in Poland as well as in the United States and elsewhere. Here in this country we received fresh encouragement in our efforts to prepare a new curriculum on teaching about the Shoah in our Catholic schools and religious education programs.

At Yad Vashem, the pope also saw the remembrances of the righteous Gentiles who had saved some from the Nazis. I was reminded of something Rabbi Marc Tanenbaum, a Baltimore native who did extraordinary interreligious work with the American Jewish Committee, told me in 1987. In Chicago he had convened a meeting of Jewish and Catholic survivors of the death camps in Poland. Almost immediately there was shouting and mutual accusations. Rabbi Tanenbaum called the group to silence and then asked each of the Jews to describe how he or she managed to survive. Everyone had been rescued by a Catholic Pole! When they realized this, the atmosphere changed. Those present realized that, with the Nazis, both Jews and Catholic Poles were victims, although the destruction of the Jewish people was their first incredible priority. One of the continuing challenges we face is the healing of memories, and Pope John Paul II's prayerful, respectful visit to Yad Vashem helped that to happen.

The pope's visit, while primarily a personal spiritual pilgrimage, meant something also to all those interested in the peace process for the region. For years he followed through on our Church's consistent teaching about war and peace, and the importance of a just peace so that families and children could live and grow preserved from an atmosphere poisoned by threat or fear. His coming offered fresh encouragement to the parties of the region to work together to resolve differences peacefully.

Yet another highly significant motif of the pilgrimage was the interreligious dimension involving Jew and Muslims in dialogue with Christians. What Pope John Paul II said to those gathered for the interfaith service will be a great legacy of his pilgrimage:

> Each of our religions knows, in some form or another, the Golden Rule: "Do unto others as you would have

them do unto you." Precious as this rule is as a guide, true love of neighbor goes much further. It is based on the conviction that when we love our neighbor we are showing love for God, and when we hurt our neighbor we offend God. This means that religion is the enemy of exclusion and discrimination, of hatred and rivalry, of violence and conflict. Religion is not, and must not become, an excuse for violence, particularly when religious identity coincides with cultural and ethnic identity. Religion and peace go together! Religious belief and practice cannot be separated from the defense of the image of God in every human being....

If the various religious communities in the Holy City and in the Holy Land succeed in living and working together in friendship and harmony, this will be of enormous benefit not only to themselves but to the whole cause of peace in this region. Jerusalem will truly be a City of Peace for all peoples. Then we will all repeat the words of the Prophet: "Come, let us go up to the mountain of the Lord...that he may teach us his ways and that we may walk in his paths" (Isa 2:3).[1]

On June 19 and 20 of 2000, the kind of dialogue between Jews and Catholics of which the pope spoke in Jerusalem took place in Washington, DC. Although most of the participants were American, the meeting had an international flavor. Rabbi Ron Kronish from Jerusalem was there, along with Father Remi Hoeckman, secretary of the Holy See's Commission for Religious Relations with the Jewish People. Rabbis from the Orthodox, Conservative, and Reform movements participated. The theme was penance and repentance in our two faith traditions. The dialogue was frank, revealing areas of difference and highlighting both the ingredients of successful dialogue and the obstacles that can block understanding and progress. For example, Catholics spoke the language in which our official Church documents are written for translation locally for some billion people around the world. It is a gentle style, quite different from the direct, sometimes strident-sounding approach more common in New York City. It is a style more subdued and peaceful, not polemical.

Words, in whatever style they are written, do not accomplish as much as deeds in advancing relationships between our faith communities. Let me cite two moments in the pope's visit to Jerusalem. One was his meeting with the two chief rabbis of Israel. In our ongoing meetings with national Jewish organizations, Dr. Fisher has commented on how startling it is, given the long, often tragic history of Catholic Jewish relations, for the successor of Peter, the leader of the apostles, to meet in dialogue, not diatribe, with respect, in dignity, and with deference, with two leaders of the heirs of the Pharisees. Neither the pope's parents nor those of the chief rabbis, Dr. Fisher noted, could have dreamed of this possibility in their wildest imaginations.

The other moment came when the pope went to the Western Wall and placed in a crevice there the prayer he had written begging God's forgiveness for the sins of Christians against Jews. Several at our June meeting here in Washington reflected that the most moving of all was the Holy Father's pause for prayer, his hand spread out upon the wall, as though he were in contact with all the Jewish suffering and all the Jewish hopes of the centuries.

We live in a sacred time. It is a time when the course of human history is changed, and for the better. It is a time when I see youth inspired by the vision of an old man who knows how to talk to them, as at Denver, Manila, Paris, and last summer in Rome. We should keep in mind a remarkable fact: This one man from Poland lived under both Nazi and Communist oppression.

Last November, at the death camp at Majdanik, just outside of Lublin, I witnessed a deeply moving service inspired by the teaching of the pope. The Romanian Orthodox patriarch, the chief rabbi of Rome, the Muslim imam of Poland, and the ranking Protestant clergyman of the land helped lead the service. I had a part, reading in English the psalm with the words, "Pray for the peace of Jerusalem." The program was televised live throughout all of Poland. All could hear the testimony of survivors that the loudspeakers carried as we walked, some 4,000 strong, from station to station in the camp. By the end, all felt the seriousness and the weight of the sad memories of the camp, and I was reminded of another reality: When Pope John Paul II was born, his land was home to the largest number of Jews in the world. When he was ordained a priest a quarter of a century later—after the Nazis had taken the lives of millions of Jews—his land was home to only a tiny remnant. This priest from Poland had now seized the opportunity not just of a lifetime but of a millennium. The world will be forever better for it.

Minneapolis, May 3, 2001

14
Covenant and Mission
The Catholic Church and the Jewish People

International Conference of Christians and Jews

It is a great joy to accept the invitation of Father John Pawlikowski, a friend for many years and companion on a historic Catholic-Jewish pilgrimage to Poland in 1992. You are already familiar with many of the positive developments that have taken place in Catholic-Jewish relations in the last four decades. My intention is to review some of them with a special emphasis on Pope John Paul II, who has been so personally dedicated to efforts to build bridges between Church and Synagogue.

Pope John Paul II has committed himself to making the teachings of the Second Vatican Council come alive in the thinking of Catholic people around the world. At the Council, Cardinal Augustin Bea introduced the first draft of what became *Nostra Aetate*, the Declaration on the Relation of the Church to Non-Christian Religions. He stood before us at the Council to speak with persuasive logic of the request of Pope John XXIII, before he died, that the Council take up this issue. Bea referred to what had occurred under Nazi rule in Europe during World War II and repeated the injunction of John XXIII that the Council should take whatever steps were necessary to be sure that never again would the Christian Scriptures or the teachings of the Church be misused in a way that might contribute to anti-Semitism.

I will focus on two of the points made by the Council as the bases for our reflection. First, although some Jews opposed the spread of the Gospel of Jesus,

> nevertheless, according to the Apostle, the Jews still remain most dear to God because of their fathers, for He does not repent of the gifts He makes nor of the calls He issues (cf. Romans 11:28–29)....Since the spiritual patrimony common to Christians and Jews is thus so great, this sacred Synod wishes to foster and recommend the mutual understanding and respect which is the fruit above all of biblical and theological studies and of brotherly dialogues. (*Nostra Aetate* 4)

Second, with specific reference to texts of the Christian Scriptures, the Council pointed out that what happened to Jesus "in his suffering cannot be blamed upon all the Jews then living, without distinction, nor upon the Jews of today" (ibid.).

This document is the basis for catechetical instruction to ensure that neither Christian Scriptures nor Christian teaching, as John XXIII said, could be used in any way that would be an excuse for anti-Semitism. And so the dream of John XXIII had been endorsed by the highest authority in the Catholic Church, the pope and bishops acting together in an ecumenical council. In the years since the Council, we have tried to apply this document to preaching in our churches, and to our teaching in seminaries, in universities, in colleges, and, perhaps most important of all, in the religious-education classes for children of every age. In the United States, we have introduced into our published liturgical resources statements that make clear not only the above but also the teaching of the Council of Trent that Jesus died because of the sins of all of us.

When Catholics think about our relationship with the Jewish people, we come to a mystery that joins Christians and Jews together. It is a mystery more fully recognized today than before the Council, but one not yet fully understood. Cardinal Walter Kasper has rightly noted that "we are at the beginning of the beginning."

I would like to carry forward this reflection, first, by speaking of the insights of *Nostra Aetate*;[1] second, by noting how Pope John Paul II developed them; and third, by offering some theological reflections that seek to take a step further so that our dialogues may be framed in a way that will relate the mystery of Jewish-Christian relations with the other dimensions of the mystery of the Church.

Nostra Aetate affirmed that in the very searching "into the mystery of the Church herself," there is to be found "that spiritual bond linking the people of the New Covenant with Abraham's stock." This compact formulation has been gradually differentiated, especially by John Paul II, whose bond with the Jewish people began in his hometown of Wadowice and his friendship with Jerzy Kluger, a Jewish boy.[2] They played together, did their homework together, and listened to records together. They both suffered the chaos of the Nazi invasion of 1939. Jurek fled after a long and difficult time. Lolek began to flee to the east with his father, just as the Red Army was marching to "liberate" Poland. He could not leave and returned to Krakow, where he worked in the mines and studied theology and, finally, was ordained a priest.

It was only in 1965 that the two friends saw each other again. The then archbishop of Krakow met Jurek in Rome where he had been living for twenty years. They spoke of the twentieth anniversary of their graduation from high school "in our old classroom on the second floor." Their farewell on that November day hints at the vision of the future pope:

They both held their hands out to shake them. But then they embraced. As Wojtyla gazed into [Jurek's] eyes, he said something that surprised his friend. Or at least something he was not expecting. "One day all Jews and Christians will be able to meet in this fashion." Kluger did not know what to say. He just said: Let's hope so. Anyway, thank you. Then with a smile: "Bye Lolek." "Bye Jurek."[3]

The vision of Pope John Paul II found its fuller account in remarks given on March 12, 1979, during his first formal presentation to an audience of representatives of Jewish organizations. There he spoke of the importance of the principles in "Guidelines and Suggestions for Implementing the Conciliar Declaration *Nostra Aetate*, no. 4," which had been developed by the Holy See.[4] He pointed to central aspects of the mystery of the relationship of Jews and Christians.

Working from the "Guidelines and Suggestions," we see that first, there is the necessity for Christians to "strive to learn by what essential traits the Jews define themselves in the light of their own religious experience." And second,

in virtue of her divine mission and her very nature, the Church must preach Jesus Christ to the world (*Ad Gentes* 2). Lest witness of Catholics to Christ should give offense to Jews, Christians must take care to live and spread their Christian faith while maintaining the strictest respect for religious liberty in line with the teaching of the Second Vatican Council in *Dignitatis Humanae*. They will likewise strive to understand the difficulties which arise for the Jewish soul—rightly imbued with an extremely high, pure notion of the divine transcendence—when faced with the mystery of the Incarnate Word.[5]

The demand made on Catholics is how to give witness to Christ by respecting the mystery that is found in the hearts and souls of Jews who are our "older brothers."

Scholars and theologians, including Cardinal Walter Kasper, president of the Pontifical Council for Promoting Christian Unity, have continued to reflect on the mystery. *Nostra Aetate* quotes St. Paul's Letter to the Romans, showing how Paul grappled with the relationship between the Christian family and the Jewish people. For Paul, it was a mystery. Two major truths were in coincidence and he sought a way to state both the tension and its resolution. And so he said that God does not call back his gifts nor repent his calls.

One statement of the question as it appeared to Catholics at the beginning of the pontificate of John Paul II was given in "Mission and Witness of the Church," a paper by Tommaso Federici for the 1977 meeting in Venice of the International Catholic-Jewish Liaison Committee. Federici emphasized the "irreversible" nature of the Church's new understanding of its relationship to the Jewish people, arguing on the basis of scriptural and magisterial sources that

> none of the inspired Christian sources justifies the notion that the Old Covenant of the Lord with His people has been abrogated or in any sense nullified.... The Church recognizes that in God's revealed plan, Israel plays a fundamental role of her own: the sanctification of the Name in the world. The Church is clear too that the honor of the Name is never unrelated to the salvation of the Jewish people who are the original nucleus of God's plan of salvation....Christ did not nullify God's plan but rather [serves] as the living and efficacious synthesis of the divine promise. [Therefore, Christian witness must take into account] the permanent place of the Jewish people according to God's plan.[6]

Pope John Paul II brought with him to the papacy a considerable experience from the pastoral sphere of his life as a worker, student, priest, and bishop under totalitarian rule. In terms of personal and official witness, he focused on the centrality of the Christian mystery of the redemption of the world through Christ in his first encyclical letter, *Redemptor Hominis* (March 4, 1979). In the encyclical *Redemptoris Missio*, presented to the Church on the twenty-fifth anniversary of Vatican II's Decree on the Church's Missionary Activity, *Ad Gentes*, he urged the Church to renew its commitment to evangelize the world, as he considered one aspect of St. Paul's concern: "Woe to me if I do not preach the Gospel." This encyclical deals with a theme that has been controversial among some Catholics since Vatican II, who considered teaching about one's faith to be merely "exporting" a foreign religion from one culture to another. The pope affirmed that the mission of the Church is part of her catholicity.

Redemptoris Missio has a special section on the relationship of mission and other religions (no. 55). Here the pope spoke to authorities in missionary countries, noting that in her preaching the Church must always respect the freedom of conscience. He wrote: "The Church proposes; she imposes nothing. She respects individuals and cultures, and she honors the sanctuary of conscience" (no. 39.2). Catholics are to undertake dialogue with a deep respect "that has been brought about in human beings by the Spirit who blows where she wills." Respect and dialogue do not permit the Church to avoid its missionary task given it by Christ, but respect and dialogue help to purify the Church and encourage greater mutual understanding among peoples and the elimination of prejudice and intolerance.

The Federici paper indicates that in the relationship with the Jewish people, the Church does not seek a proselytism that focuses on the Jewish people. In his understanding of the central issues noted in his first meeting with Jewish leaders in 1979, John Paul II knew well the difference between proselytizing and evangelizing in mission. For the mystery of mission of the relation of the Catholic Church and the Jewish people holds together simultaneously the issues of religious freedom, the Church's responsibility for her mission, and the eternality of the Jewish Covenant. Since the Second Vatican Council, the Church has neither established nor sanctioned any organizations designed for the conversion of Jews. In 1996, Cardinal John O'Connor of New York joined with Protestant Church executives in affirming that this is the basic approach of the post-Holocaust Christian family of Churches. Of course, there are exceptions, who read New Testament passages so as not to account for the creative tension expressed by St. Paul in Romans 11.

Lex orandi, lex credendi. There is only one official prayer for the Jews in our Catholic liturgy, the traditional Good Friday prayer. It is in the middle of a threefold prayer for the Church (*fideles*, believers), for the Jews (*perfideles*, half believers), and for unbelievers (*infideles*). Over the centuries, the teaching of contempt burdened the original theological category of *perfideles* with so much opprobrium that the modern term *perfidious* took on a far more sinister meaning than first intended by the ancient liturgy. In the mid-1950s, Pope Pius XII directed that *perfideles* no longer be translated as "perfidious" but rather as "unbelieving" or "unfaithful." Blessed John XXIII ordered that the Latin term be deleted from the prayer altogether, though it remained a prayer for the conversion of Jews.

The reform of the Good Friday liturgy mandated by the Second Vatican Council reconceptualized and rewrote the prayer entirely. It now reads:

> Let us pray for the Jewish people, the first to hear the word of God, that they may continue to grow in the love of his Name and in faithfulness to his covenant. Almighty and eternal God, long ago you gave your promise to Abraham and his posterity. Listen to your

Church as we pray that the people you first made your own may arrive at the fullness of redemption.

The phrase *fullness of redemption* is blessed with ambiguity. It should be seen not as historical but as eschatological. Like St. Paul in Romans 11, the phrase leaves the issue in God's hands, to be revealed at the end of time with the Second Coming of Christ, redeemer of all humanity. Of course, individual Jews whose own spiritual lives and consciences lead them to fullness of our faith are welcomed into the Church. To do otherwise would offend against the principles of religious freedom and of mission.

The most significant of John Paul II's prayers regarding the Jews is the one he prayed first at the millennial liturgy of repentance in Rome and placed in the Western Wall in Jerusalem, affirming in the strongest way possible the Church's opposition to anti-Semitism and its eternal debt to Judaism for having given us the revelation of God. Less well known, but also theologically significant, is his prayer for the Jews composed at the request of the bishops of Poland in 1998, and now prayed throughout the country on Poland's annual day of reflection on Jews and Judaism. It serves as a model for how Catholics should pray for the Jews.

God of Abraham, the prophets, [and] Jesus Christ, in you everything is embraced, toward you everything moves, you are the end of all things. Hear the prayers we extend for the Jewish nation, which— thanks to its forefathers—is still very dear to you.

Instill within it a constant, ever livelier desire to deepen your truth and love. Help it, as it yearns for peace and justice, that it may reveal to the world the might of your blessing.

Succor it that it may obtain respect and love from the side of those who do not yet understand the greatness of suffering it has borne, and those who, in solidarity and a sense of mutual care, experience together the pain of wounds inflicted upon it.

Remember the new generations of youth and children that they may, unchangeably faithful to you, uphold what remains the particular mystery of their vocation.

Strengthen all generations, that, thanks to their testimony, humanity will understand that your salvific intention extends over all the human family, and that you, God, are for all nations the beginning and the final end.

𑁍

[Editor's note: Following is the final section of this same address by Cardinal Keeler.]

THE UNIVERSAL MISSION OF THE CHURCH AND THE JEWISH PEOPLE

In the United States, one of the fruits of the ongoing dialogue between scholars selected by the National Council of Synagogues and the U.S. Catholic Bishops' Committee for Ecumenical and Interreligious Affairs is the publication of "Reflections on Covenant and Mission."[7] Although representing solely the work of the scholars involved and not an official text of either institution, the work has given rise to considerable discussion. As Cardinal Walter Kasper of the Holy See's Commission for Religious Relations with the Jews has pointed out, the publication opened the way to a more profound theological discussion between Catholics and Jews.

It is useful to note that the term *covenant* must be seen as not universal in meaning. It does not indicate a clearly defined and universally recognized reality. It is important to remember that the Hebrew Scriptures speak of different types of covenant according to the situation and the persons involved, for example, the covenant with Noah in Genesis 9, the covenant with Abraham in Genesis 17, and the covenant on Sinai in Exodus 19–24, 32–34. Jeremiah 31:31 even mentions a "new covenant" that refers to the content of the Sinitic one but implies a completely new orientation, that the Law is now written in the hearts of the Israelites so that it cannot be broken any more. The fundamental meaning of this covenant is expressed through the words: "I will be their God and they shall be my people." The covenant does not guarantee automatic salvation but offers the possibility of partaking in salvation. Therefore, those who follow God's indications contained in it, who are faithful to the Torah, have the correct relationship with God and can receive the gift of salvation from God.

The Bible presents not only different examples of covenant, but also different conceptions of it, such as the Deuteronomic idea based on the old oriental contracts, and also the priestly idea according to which there is only God's salvific proposal, which humanity simply needs to accept. *Covenant* never means a legal or juridical contract between two partners with equal rights that can be used as the basis for human claims. The initiative always comes from God and cannot be forced by individual men and women. Because of these different types and ideas of covenant, there are different ways in which the word *covenant* (in Hebrew *b'rit*) is used in the Bible, so that this word is never univocal and unidimensional. Note also the parallelism between the words *covenant* and *election*, which sometimes simply means a special relationship with God. The conclusion that can be drawn from these points is that the theological discussion following "Reflections on Covenant and Mission" should give greater weight to the biblical dimension of the concept of covenant. It seems necessary to deepen the understanding of this word and see which theological dimensions are bound into it.

In an address titled "The Commission for Religious Relations with the Jews: A Crucial Endeavour of the Catholic

Church," given at Boston College in 2002, Cardinal Kasper presented guidelines on how to relate the overall mission to proclaim the Good News universally while at the same time acknowledging the profound particularity of its unique relationship with God's people, Israel. Cardinal Kasper said:[8]

> This issue is not a new one, and has been debated for a long time in our dialogues. But it does touch on the fundamental question which stands between us, and in that perspective new reflections and fresh ideas are welcome, although clearly easy answers are not possible. As I see things, a convincing solution is not yet in sight and the discussion must continue. Thus, I take this document [on Covenant and Mission] for what it sets itself out to be, and that is, an invitation and a challenge for further discussion. What I have to say is certainly not definitive, and represents no more than a modest personal contribution to a still unresolved problem.

Acknowledging that discussing Christian missionary activity will evoke for Jews painful historical memories of forced conversions, Kasper unequivocally stated the rejection of such efforts by the Church today and her sense of repentance for them, citing the Second Vatican Council's Declaration on Religious Liberty, *Dignitatis Humanae*, with its "rejection of all means of coercion in matters of faith and regarding the recognition of religious freedom." The question, he said, must be approached with great sensitivity. But he noted that the issue must be raised, since mission and witness are part of Christian identity:

> The word "mission" is central in the New Testament. We cannot cancel it, and if we should try to do so, it would not help the Jewish-Christian dialogue at all.

Rather, it would make the dialogue dishonest, and ultimately distort it. If Jews want to speak with Christians they cannot demand that Christians no longer be Christians. This is the very essence of dialogue—neither confusion nor absorption, or relativism or syncretism, but encounter of different perspectives and horizons, and—as I have learned from Jewish thinkers like Martin Buber and Emmanuel Levinas—recognition of the other in his/her otherness.

The issue bears on the essence of that which is common and that which divides us, at the core of our respective identities:

What we have in common is above all what Jews call the Hebrew Bible and we the Old Testament. We have in common our common father in faith Abraham, and Moses and the Ten Commandments, the Patriarchs and Prophets, the covenant and the promises of the one and unique God, and the messianic hope. Because we have all this in common and because as Christians we know that God's covenant with Israel by God's faithfulness is not broken (Rom. 11, 29; cf. 3.4), mission [that is] understood as a call to conversion from idolatry to the living and true God (1 Thess. 1, 9) does not apply and cannot be applied to Jews. They confess the living true God, who gave and gives them support, hope, confidence and strength in many difficult situations of their history. There cannot be the same kind of behavior towards Jews as there exists towards Gentiles. This is not a merely abstract theological affirmation, but an affirmation that has concrete and tangible consequences such as the fact that there is no organized Catholic missionary activity towards Jews.

Kasper also noted that the differences between Judaism and Christianity come to the fore immediately in the names we give our shared Scriptures: Hebrew Bible or Old Testament, which indicates differing interpretations of what we have in common. Paradoxically we could say that we differ on what we have in common. The Pontifical Biblical Commission's statement *The Jewish People and Their Sacred Scriptures in the Christian Bible*[9] (2001) affirms that both interpretations, Jewish rabbinical and Christian, are possible and legitimate, depending on our faith perspective. Jews, Kasper noted, await the coming of the Messiah while we Christians await his return. Citing Ephesians 2:14–18; Colossians 1:15–18; 1 Timothy 2:5; and Romans 3:24 and 8:32— Kasper emphasized that for Christians all humans, Jews and Gentiles alike, will be saved through Christ: "From the Christian perspective the covenant with the Jewish people is unbroken (Rom. 11:29), for we as Christians believe that these promises find in Jesus their definitive and irrevocable Amen (2 Cor. 1:20) and at the same time that in him, who is the end of the law (Rom 10:4), the law is not nullified but upheld (Rom 3:31)." And here he added an all-important caveat:

> This does not mean that Jews in order to be saved have to become Christians; if they follow their own conscience and believe in God's promises as they understand them in their religious tradition they are in line with God's plan, which for us comes to its historical completion in Jesus Christ.

Romans 9–11 with its affirmation of the irrevocable nature of God's covenant with the Jews (Rom 11:29) provides, as *Nostra Aetate* affirmed, the context for understanding Christian mission with regard to the Jews, just as other conciliar documents and the use made by Pope John Paul II of *Nostra Aetate*, for example, the encyclical *Redemptoris Missio* (I 990), provide the context today for reading the conciliar declaration.

Kasper concluded his remarks at Boston College with a note on the historical context of the present dialogue: "Much is to be undertaken....Here we are only at the beginning of a new beginning."

I must be candid to admit that we Catholics have much to do to render our speech, both unofficially and officially, much more consistent and clear than it now is. But, just as deeply, I am persuaded that the doctrinal understanding outlined by Cardinal Kasper represents a helpful first step for the future of Catholic teaching.

Utrecht, Netherlands, July 2, 2003

15

The Passion of the Christ Revisited

The Catholic Review

In the annual Lenten letter, I suggested that it could be helpful to see Mel Gibson's film *The Passion of the Christ* with a person of another faith background and to discuss afterward what was seen and its meaning for those who watched. As I wrote then, many who had seen it, Catholics all, told me how deeply impressed they were by its power to convey the extent of Christ's sufferings and the depth of his love for us. Some others, who had not seen it, expressed reservations and concerns about the film as a possible source of anti-Semitism. When I first saw it, I was overwhelmed by the vivid depiction of the physical violence inflicted on Jesus and so missed much of the detail.

From priests and laity alike, I have heard how an increase in attendance at the sacraments, the Holy Week services, and the Stations of the Cross was attributed to people having seen the film. In Baltimore and elsewhere, parishioners spoke to me of the spiritual reinforcement they found in the movie.

And then, at a meeting in New York, Jewish leaders told me of their heightened concerns and even fears. Thus, last week I took my own advice and saw the movie with a rabbi and a well-informed Jewish layperson, both of them articulate and sensitive. While I had heard and read criticisms before, this second viewing opened my eyes to aspects of the film I had not caught previously, and I saw why our Jewish neighbors view it with understandable concern and even a measure of fear.

After seeing the picture, we talked about it and its context in our increasingly secular society. For this conversation, the rabbi's wife joined us. She too had seen the film. For many Christians, I observed, the movie represents a breakthrough—an opportunity for faith values to be reflected on the screen in a way that has a broad appeal. I told the others present of the positive impact the film had had on many of our people. Father Rob Jaskot, from my office, shared his impressions also. Sitting with our Jewish friends, we both told of having seen a different picture.

Even though Jesus, his mother, the apostles, and indeed all in the picture whom we identify as "Christians" were Jewish, the depiction of the Temple leaders and the crowd left impressions that, we saw, could be twisted in an anti-Semitic way. Our active Catholic people, those who regularly participate in Mass and hear the Church's preaching, know full well that Jesus bore the sins of us all. So also, the Catholics who have seen no anti-Semitism in the film have interpreted it according to their understanding of the Gospels and of the artistic creativity used in interpreting the Gospel accounts.

We spoke of what is happening now on the Internet, with anti-Catholic and anti-Semitic Web sites everywhere. I told them what many of our Catholics feel, namely, that anti-Catholicism may be an even more pressing problem than anti-Semitism in the United States. It was agreed that a certain Christian faction is still very anti-Catholic and also that the secular side of our society is pressing in on all people of faith.

Christians and others who are predisposed to prejudice against Catholics and Jews *could* take from this movie an anti-Semitic viewpoint. Sadly, we agreed, in Arab countries and in places in Europe where there has been strong anti-Semitism in the past, the movie can cause harm. I can see where our Jewish partners in dialogue would be worried, even fearful, of evil possibly resulting from a Christian viewing this film unprepared. They spoke of some individual cases in the United States where Jewish children were spoken to abusively by some Christian youths. We agreed in hoping that genuine good can be accomplished through discussion and joint Catholic-Jewish statements, as we look together for the reconciliation and peace so much sought after by Pope John Paul II.

On Monday morning I was privileged to meet with the Holy Father, to introduce to him the auxiliary bishops and our priests studying in Rome. Privately, we discussed issues before our people in Baltimore. To our Catholic people he sends his special blessing. And to our many Jewish neighbors he asked me to convey his warm good wishes.

Baltimore, April 28, 2004

16
Reflections on Anti-Semitism and the Church[1]

The first half of the twentieth century was arguably the most violent and tragic period in human history. Two World Wars devastated much of the globe. Advances in technology enabled totalitarian regimes to destroy entire populations. Indeed, a new vocabulary with words such as *genocide* and *Holocaust* had to be developed to describe the horrors visited on whole peoples in so many parts of the world.

The second half of the twentieth century saw new beginnings and renewed hopes, as new nations arose and democratic principles began to spread to lands that had long been suffering under oppression. Among Christians, the ecumenical movement articulated the deep longing for unity. Between Christians and people of other religions, dialogue began to replace disputation, a process whose spirit was embodied in the gathering at Assisi in 1986 of the leaders of the world's great religions to pray for reconciliation and peace. Similarly, the prayerful visit of Pope John Paul II to the Great Synagogue of Rome earlier in the same year vividly exemplified the Church's attitude of respect for the Jewish people and for Judaism, as did his liturgy of repentance in St. Peter's in Rome and his subsequent visit to Yad Vashem and the Western Wall (*Kotel*) in Jerusalem in 2000.

For Catholics, the impetus for involvement in these move-ments of the Spirit came chiefly from the Second Vatican Council in the 1960s, which condemned both anti-Semitism and Christian theological polemics, and called for "fraternal dialogues" with Jews.[2] The Holy See's Commission for Religious Relations with the Jews was established after the Council to implement this vision and has issued three major statements.[3] Also, it has cosponsored a series of international dialogues with representatives of the Jewish people.

At the same time, episcopal conferences around the world have issued statements and guidelines to foster understanding of Jews and Judaism among Catholics. Central in all of these offi-cial Catholic reflections, including *Nostra Aetate*, as the 1985 guidelines affirmed, has been the necessity to preserve "the mem-ory of the persecution and massacre of Jews which took place in Europe just before and during the Second World War."

Pope John Paul II has repeatedly called upon Catholics "to see where we stand" in our historic relationship with the Jewish people.[4] In doing so, we must remember how much the balance (of these relations) over two thousand years has been negative.[5] This very long period, "which we must not tire of reflecting upon in order to draw from it the appropriate lessons,"[6] has been marked by many manifestations of anti-Semitism and, in the last century, by the terrible events of the Shoah.[7] In meeting with Jewish lead-ers at the beginning of his September 1987 pastoral visit to the United States, the pope referred to the Shoah and called for the development of "common educational programs" to "promote mutual respect and teach future generations about the Holocaust so that never again will such a horror be possible. Never again!"[8]

"There is no future without memory."[9] Memory and memories are crucial for understanding Jewish-Christian relationships in the past and for the future. *Memoria futuri*. Memories need to be approached with great sensitivity and care for the truth, which is often complex and ambiguous. How did European civilization, largely Christian for so many centuries, reach the point where there could emerge and prevail such a profoundly un-Christian and, indeed, anti-Christian idea as dividing the one human race into groups perceived as subhuman? I say "anti-Christian" because of the Christian teaching that every man and woman is infinitely precious as made in "the image of God." And how then could European civilization slate those groups for elimination as though they were less than human? Why the fanatical focus on the Jews? Why was the opposition of civil, intellectual, and religious leaders so ineffectual? Why did the rest of the world look on and, with very few exceptions, refuse to provide life-saving refuge? Why did the genocidal hatred against God's people, the Jews, emerge in the twentieth century and not before, for example, in medieval times, when the Church had more political power?

These and many other questions are raised by the history of the past centuries. They still concern us today. They concern the whole of humanity. They concern the Church. It is greatly encouraging to note, in this context, the development of so many centers and institutions of Christian-Jewish studies, many connected to Catholic universities, both in Europe and the United States. These have joined to form the Council of Centers of Jewish-Christian Relations, which will enable them to share research and respond to new developments.[10]

One of the reasons for the urgency of confronting the Shoah in Catholic thinking today lies in the question of whether there exists a relationship between the modern racial anti-Semitism propounded by National Socialism in the 1920s and '30s, and the negative images of Jews and Judaism encrusted on Christian teaching itself over the centuries. And if there is a relationship, we ask, how ought it to be understood? And how do we inoculate future generations of Catholics against its reemergence?

The great French Jewish historian Jules Isaac was one of the first to study this issue in a systematic way, beginning his studies even as he hid from the Nazis during World War II.[11] His work showed that, very early in the history of the Church, passages of the

New Testament—which had originally been written in the context of what was then an internal Jewish controversy between the Evangelists, who were Jewish, and other Jewish leaders—were taken out of that context by Christian Gentiles of subsequent generations, embroidered with already-existing Greco-Roman anti-Jewish rhetoric, and then "read back" into the New Testament, creating a systematic distortion that he aptly called "the teaching of contempt" against Jews and Judaism. Cardinal Joseph Ratzinger, in introducing the 2001 document of the Pontifical Biblical Commission, *The Jewish People and Their Sacred Scriptures in the Christian Bible*,[12] asks the question: "Did not the presentation of the Jews and of the Jewish people, in the New Testament itself, contribute to creating a hostility to this people which the ideology of those who wanted to suppress it has encouraged?" This document and that of the Holy See's Commission for Religious Relations with the Jews (*We Remember: A Reflection on the Shoah*, 1998) candidly admit the historical link between the ancient and modern forms of anti-Semitism. The Pontifical Biblical Commission states that many passages in the New Testament that are critical of the Jews "served as a pretext for anti-Jewish sentiment and, effectively, have been used for this purpose" (no. 87), while *We Remember* acknowledges that "sentiments of anti-Judaism in some Christian quarters, and the gap which existed between the Church and the Jewish people, led to a generalized discrimination" toward the Jews over the centuries, in particular in Christian Europe.[13]

Over the centuries, the anti-Jewish teaching was refined, developed, and made ever-more negative until, in the twentieth century, the majority of Christians in Europe had such a negative (and false!) understanding of Judaism and such a negative attitude toward Jews that they became easy prey for the Nazi racial categorizations that rationalized genocide. Within Christianity, Pope John Paul II has noted:

erroneous and unjust interpretations of the New
Testament relative to the Jewish people and their pre-
sumed guilt circulated for too long, engendering sentiments of hostility toward this people. That contributed
to the lulling of many consciences, so that when Europe
was swept by the wave of persecutions inspired by a
pagan anti-Semitism that in its essence was equally
anti-Christian, alongside those Christians who did
everything to save those who were persecuted, even to
the point of risking their own lives, the spiritual resist-
ance of many was not what humanity expected from
Christ's disciples.[14]

This framing of the issue, while acknowledging fully the historical link between Christian anti-Judaism and Nazi anti-Semitism,
also acknowledges the distinctions between them. Distinctions are
necessary for the historical record. Christian anti-Judaism was not
racial in character. For example, it adhered to the teaching of Genesis
on the oneness of humanity in the divine image,[15] and sought a vision
of the Church itself in which the distinction between Jew and Gentile
would be overcome by baptism.[16] History, too, shows the difference.
Historian Yosef Yerushalmi asked why, if genocide had been latent
in the Christian teaching of contempt, no such attempt was made in
the Middle Ages when the Church held sufficient political power
within "Christendom" to implement such an idea:

There is no question but that Christian anti-Semitism
through the ages helped create the climate and men-
tality in which genocide, once conceived, could be
achieved with little or no opposition. But even if we
grant that Christian teaching was a necessary cause
leading to the Holocaust, it was surely not a sufficient
one. The Holocaust was the work of a thoroughly
modern, neo-pagan (secularist) state....The slaughter

of the Jews by the state was not part of the medieval Christian world order. It became possible with the breakdown of that order.[17]

It does not diminish the failures and sins of Christians on all levels in Church and society over the centuries to acknowledge the multiplicity of causes that led to the unthinkable becoming reality in the twentieth century. Today we must, for the sake of future generations, confront all the causes that led to the Holocaust so that, in understanding them, we can effectively ensure that nothing similar can ever occur again, whether to Jews or to other peoples. It is vital to continue the work of the Second Vatican Council to reject and to eliminate from Catholic teaching anything that might be used to present the Jews "as repudiated by God or accursed, as if this followed from Sacred Scripture."[18] As John Paul II said:

> For Christians the heavy burden of guilt for the murder of the Jewish people must be an enduring call to repentance. Through it we can overcome every form of anti-Semitism and establish a new relationship with our kindred nation of the Old Covenant. The Church, mindful of her common patrimony with the Jews, and motivated by the Gospels' spiritual love...deplores the hatred, persecutions, and displays of anti-Semitism directed against the Jews at any time and from any source (*Nostra Aetate*, n. 4). Guilt should not oppress and lead to self-agonizing, but must always be the point of departure for conversion.[19]

The failure and guilt of that time have a Church dimension. Despite the exemplary behavior of many Christian individuals and groups, most Christians kept on living their lives—in essence turning their back on the fate of their Jewish neighbors, looking fixedly at the threat to their own institutions, and remaining all too often silent. Though the Shoah was conceived and carried out by a thoroughly "modern" neo-pagan regime, the classical teaching of contempt was a central factor in "lulling the consciences" of Christians, in enabling them to remain appallingly indifferent to Jewish suffering, and even in generating popular support among many for the Nazi crimes. Thus it happened that Jewish men, women, and children were systematically put to death without the Christian community as a whole raising a successful and effective opposition.

The fact that throughout history and during the Shoah many people in the Church, leaders as well as ordinary faithful, did speak up and act in defense of the Jews at the risk of their lives (for example, the convents and monasteries of Italy in which, in response to the personal leadership of Pope Pius XII, thousands of Jews were hidden during the Nazi occupation)[20] does not take away the guilt of those other Christians, leaders as well as ordinary faithful, who committed the sin of anti-Semitism by action or omission. God will judge them.

Already in 1988, the Holy See's Commission for Justice and Peace, in its document "The Church and Racism," noted that "anti-Zionism—which is not of the same order [as anti-Semitism], since it questions the State of Israel and its policies—serves at times as a screen for anti-Semitism, feeding on it and leading to it."[21] Old conspiracy theories and world domination fantasies are being given new life and are exploiting the conflict between Israel and the Palestinians.

In January of 2004, the European Monitoring Centre on Racism and Xenophobia completed a study, begun in 2002, of "Manifestations of Anti-Semitism in the European Union," which concluded that while the familiar threat by "ordinary" right-wing anti-Semitism is obvious, left-wing, anti-globalization, Muslim, and pro-Palestinian groups are backbones of contemporary anti-Semitism as well. At the same time, I do wish to note some cautions about the Middle East situation. One is the fact that the Christians living there, living in Israel and under the Palestinian Authority, feel themselves under constant pressure.

As Father Drew Christiansen has pointed out, there has been a lack of effective police involvement in protecting Christians and their holy sites in Nazareth and other places. The lack of police action in Nazareth, whether in protecting Christians against attack or in preventing illegal construction, is a recurrent problem. When the militants rioted a few years ago, attacking Christians, the police held back for three days before intervening in the fray. Sometime later, the police commander for the northern region admitted that he had been under orders not to get involved. With repeated court orders and top government decisions to end the construction in Nazareth, it is hard to comprehend how the authorities could have permitted the protest site to become half completed. Under such conditions, you can understand why the Christians of Galilee live in fear.

The vulnerability of Israel's indigenous Christians is made apparent in the vulnerability of the holy places. Just like the illegal construction in Nazareth, the occupation and siege [some time ago] of the Church of the Nativity in Bethlehem revealed the pressures to which the Holy Land's Christians are now exposed. In both cases they found themselves and the holy places at the mercy of the worst of their neighbors, along with outside agitators. Before the al-Aqsa intifada, there were some 50,000 Christians on the West Bank. Today, as a result of emigration, there are fewer than 35,000. The ambiguities in police protection, whether by the Palestinian Authority or the Israeli police, including the border police, are a source of grave concern for the future of the Church in the Holy Land.

Also, there is the issue of the Latin Patriarch, Michel Sabbah. As Father Christiansen pointed out:

> Patriarch Sabbah is a Palestinian National, but he is also a bishop with responsibilities after Vatican II—and I would add after World War II and the Holocaust—to speak out on issues of justice, peace and human rights.

When asked, he consults with police officials on some security matters. With the Anglican and Lutheran bishops, both Palestinians, he has gone to Gaza to meet with Sheikh Yassin, the spiritual head of Hamas, to ask him to end suicide bombings. He has met...with Israel's chief rabbis, in an unprecedented move for a Middle East Christian leader, and he engages in regular bible study with rabbis and priests of the Patriarchate. Because of this he is shunned, as I was alarmed to discover, by even moderate, secular academics of Muslim background.... When he called for political leaders who could not bring peace to step aside, he once again was criticized by the Palestinian side. But he is given no credit by Israel. Instead he is scorned by an [Israeli] official with an important role in interreligious relations as "the Islamic Patriarch." The issues of fairness and of honest respect deserve to be raised in this context. Anything that we can do to promote both fairness and honest respect among leaders will help to hasten the day of justice and peace in the land we call Holy.[22]

In Europe, there has been a huge increase in anti-Semitic speech and incidents, the latter in the main attributed to young Arabs influenced by anti-Israel propaganda. European governments, to their credit, are now taking the rise over the last three years quite seriously, though they did not seem to initially. On April 28, 2004, over five hundred representatives from the fifty-five-nation Organization for Security and Cooperation in Europe convened in Berlin to formulate an action plan to deal with the growing problem throughout Europe. Secretary of State Colin Powell represented the United States, acknowledging candidly that "regrettably, my own country has its share of anti-Semites, skinheads and other assorted racists, bigots and extremists, who feed on fear and ignorance and prey on the vulnerable."

One very distressing feature of the new anti-Semitism is the use in Muslim countries of so much of the remnants of Christian anti-Semitism, such as the widespread distribution of translations of the thoroughly discredited "classics" *The Protocols of the Elders of Zion* and *The Talmud Unmasked*. Similarly, in some parts of the Arab world, certain elements of the Gibson movie that derive from pre–Vatican II passion plays have been exploited for anti-Israel and anti-Semitic propaganda. I would hope that the United Nations, which will hold its first-ever seminar on anti-Semitism on June 21, 2004, will confront the phenomenon not only in its "old" but also its "new" form as well.

The Catholic Church takes the rise in anti-Semitism very seriously. When, some three years ago, the situation appeared on the verge of getting out of hand in France, and the politicians were silent because it was an election year and they seemed unwilling to alienate French Muslim voters, the French Bishops' Conference issued a terse, strongly worded statement condemning anti-Semitism that broke the logjam and allowed the politicians to find their own voices and actions. Last fall, Cardinal Walter Kasper, the president of the Pontifical Commission for Religious Relations with the Jews, felt it necessary to publish, in the October 1 edition of *L'Osservatore Romano*, an article he had written entitled "Anti-Semitism: A Wound to Be Healed."[23] Cardinal Kasper reminded his readers to be ever alert for signs of anti-Semitism and to probe its history and causes even within our own Christian teaching, in order to root it out once and for all.

We need to be concerned not only about the cultural, social, political, ideological, and more generally "secular" dimensions of anti-Semitism, but also about a specific aspect of it that was firmly condemned in 1928 by the Apostolic See when it defined anti-Semitism as *"odium adversus populum olim a Deo electum"* ("hatred against a people once chosen by God") (*AAS* XX/1928, 103–4). Today, seventy-five years later, the only modification we feel duty bound to make is the elimination of the word *olim* ("once").

This is no small thing, because in recognizing the perennial timeliness of the covenant between God and his people Israel, we in turn will be able to rediscover, with our Jewish brethren, the irrevocable universality of the vocation to serve humanity in peace and in justice, until the definitive coming of his kingdom. This is what the Pope John Paul II also recommended to us in his post-synodal apostolic exhortation *Ecclesia in Europa*[24] of last June, recalling

> the *relationship which binds the Church to the Jewish people* and of Israel's unique role in salvation history....There is need for acknowledgment of the common roots linking Christianity and the Jewish people, who are called by God to a covenant which remains irrevocable (cf. Rom 11:29) and has attained definitive fullness in Christ. Consequently, it is necessary to encourage dialogue with Judaism, knowing that it is fundamentally important for the self-knowledge of Christians and for the transcending of divisions between the Churches. (no. 56)

Dialogue and collaboration between Christians and Jews also implies that "acknowledgment be given to any part which the children of the Church have had in the growth and spread of anti-Semitism in history; forgiveness must be sought for this from God, and every effort must be made to favor encounters of reconciliation and of friendship with the sons of Israel" (no. 56). In this spirit of rediscovered brotherhood, a new springtime for the Church and for the world can bloom once more, with the heart turned from Rome to Jerusalem and to the land of the Fathers, so that there too a just and lasting peace may quickly germinate for all and mature like a banner flying in the midst of the peoples.

Salvador, Brazil, June 6, 2004

17
A Developing Agenda for Catholic-Jewish Dialogue[1]

The agenda for dialogue between Catholics and Jews has been rather remarkably constant since its early days at the time of the Second Vatican Council. One of the first formal dialogues in the United States, for example, was held at St. Vincent's Archabbey in Latrobe, Pennsylvania, in January of 1965, almost a year before the issuance of the document *Nostra Aetate*. The papers from that dialogue, edited by Philip Scharper, were published by Sheed and Ward in 1966 under the title *Torah and Gospel: Jewish and Catholic Theology in Dialogue*. The table of contents of that classic collection of seminal essays in the field remains even today a suitable frame for considering much of the future agenda of Catholic-Jewish relations, although a wealth of literature in each category since then has greatly enriched the Church's understanding of the deeper issues involved.

Leading this discussion at Latrobe were Rabbi Solomon Grayzel of Brandeis University and Father John Sheerin, CSP, editor of *The Catholic World*. The starting point in the discussion was the thesis set forth by French historian and Holocaust survivor Jules Isaac, whose classic works of the 1940s in the field, *Jesus and Israel* and *The Teaching of Contempt: Christian Roots of Anti-Semitism*, were translated into English only in the early 1960s by Claire Hutchet Bishop. These publications helped pave

111

the way for the Council's declaration. The two scholars agreed with Isaac's contention that the ancient Christian "teaching of contempt" against Jews and Judaism went back to the earliest Fathers of the Church and must be uprooted from Christian theology lest the tragedies of history repeat themselves. But they parted company over two key issues with a distinctly contemporary ring.

Whereas Grayzel, following Isaac, sought to place the beginning of the teaching of contempt within the New Testament itself, Sheerin, following Catholic scholar Gregory Baum, argued that it was rooted not in the New Testament but in "misunderstandings" of the New Testament by Christians beginning in the second century. One can see the nuanced language preferred by Sheerin in 1965 echoed in statements by Pope John Paul II and in the Holy See's 1998 statement *We Remember: A Reflection on the Shoah*. It is important to note that the "anti-Jewish" polemics in the New Testament originally reflected internal disputes in the decades after Jesus' time, between the Jews who believed in him and those who did not accept the claims about him. In Jesus' own time, as the Pontifical Biblical Commission's statement *The Jewish People and Their Sacred Scriptures in the Christian Bible* (2001) makes clear, few Jews aside from the leadership of the Temple priesthood would have opposed Jesus.

The second difference between Rabbi Grayzel's and Father Sheerin's views is that the former, although taking a nuanced view of history that acknowledged both the papal protectiveness of Jews over the centuries, as well as its many periods of tolerance, insisted along with Isaac that Nazi anti-Semitism was in continuity with ancient Christian anti-Semitism and was in fact its culmination, if not its inevitable one. Sheerin, on the other hand, cited Charles Journet, Gregory Baum, and Henri de Lubac to the effect that "Hitlerian anti-Semitism had no roots in Christian preaching or teaching," though he did allow that "Christian preaching has created a type of Jew whose image has entered the Christian sub-

`

conscious, producing a psychological mechanism of which pagan hate can take possession."[2]

Today, I believe we would hold the two, continuity and discontinuity, in more equal balance. While distinguishing between Christian polemics against Judaism and Jews over the centuries on the one hand, and the modern racial, genocidal anti-Semitism of the Nazis on the other, the U.S. bishops' document *Catholic Teaching on the Shoah* also insists on the historical continuity between them.

> The Christian teaching of anti-Judaism (leading to anti-Jewishness)…is a "necessary cause" to consider in explaining the development and success of [Nazi anti-Semitism] in the twentieth century—but not a 'sufficient cause.' To account for the Holocaust, one must acknowledge the historical role of Christian anti-Judaism. But Christian anti-Judaism alone cannot account for the Holocaust. Semi-scientific racial theories and specific historical, ideological, economic and social realities within Germany must also be taken into account.[3]

Forty years after Latrobe and the Second Vatican Council, we are, sadly, experiencing a renewed anti-Semitism in which, as the statement *The Church and Racism*[4] of the Pontifical Council for Justice and Peace warned as long ago as 1988, anti-Zionism is being used by certain intellectual circles in both the left and right and in both Europe and the Americas "as a screen for anti-Semitism, feeding on it and leading to it." This has been dubbed the "new anti-Semitism," but it is really not so new. What is, perhaps, new is its particular virulence in parts of the Muslim world, where old results of Western anti-Semitism such as the *Protocols of the Elders of Zion* and *The Talmud Unmasked* are being widely circulated. What is also new, in post-Shoah Europe, is the sharp rise in not only anti-Semitic rhetoric but anti-Semitic incidents. So seriously is this taken that the European Union has itself initiated international studies and meetings to analyze and counter it.

One of the most significant areas of progress made by the Second Vatican Council was the reform of our Catholic liturgy. One of the most significant sources of insight for this reform, in turn, was the rediscovery by Catholic scholars of the Jewish roots of our liturgy.[5] At Latrobe, Rabbi Solomon Freeh of Hebrew Union College and Father Aidan Kavanagh, OSB, of St. Meinrad Seminary ably recounted the cross-fructification of Jewish and Christian liturgical traditions over the centuries. Here again solid foundations have been laid in the four decades since these talks were given. But much more work needs to be done. The reform of Catholic liturgy with respect to its traditionally negative portrayal of Jews and Judaism is not yet complete. The Good Friday prayer for the conversion of the "perfidious Jews" has been radically altered into a respectful prayer that God will intensify the Jews in their faithful response to His ongoing covenant with them. But this does not exhaust the challenges faced by Catholic liturgists. The passion is still read without official commentary or guidance on Passion Sunday and Good Friday, leaving it up to local churches and pastors to "fill in" how it is to be understood by their congregations. Numerous questions about selections of lectionary texts abound. Often, it is difficult in the juxtaposition of biblical texts to distinguish between a theological relationship of fulfillment (the Church's teaching that Jesus fulfilled the biblical promises, though we await their "perfect fulfillment" at the end of time), and supersessionism (the idea that the Church has replaced Judaism as the people of God, which was declared a heresy by the Church in the second century of the Common Era. More profound changes will come within the Roman liturgy itself, but only when Catholic liturgists sit down seriously with Catholics and Jews who have worked together on these issues over the years in national and international dialogues.

Likewise of importance for the agenda facing us today is more serious work by Jewish scholars on Jewish liturgy. Certain aspects of Jewish worship, for example, the medieval *piyyutim* or daily prayers, were developed in times of tension between Jews and Christians, and can be read, though phrased more subtly, as polemics against Christianity that mislead Jewish worshipers as to the true nature of Christian faith and practice. And I believe much more work needs to be done to surface and acknowledge areas of Jewish life and worship that have been deeply influenced by Christianity over the centuries. Some work has been done in this area.[6] But I would suggest that a smaller percentage of educated Jews are aware of Christian influences on Jewish liturgy than educated Catholics are aware of the Jewish origins of their liturgical practices.

The burgeoning of interactive Catholic and Jewish biblical scholarship has been one of the great achievements of the post–Vatican II era. Here, Rabbi Samuel Sandmel of Hebrew Union College and Father Roland Murphy, O.Carm., of the Catholic University of America presaged a solid generation of tremendously exciting interaction. Today, it is common for Jewish scholars to publish articles in *Catholic Biblical Quarterly* and for CBQ to review Jewish books. Indeed, the book review editor for *New* Testament and Intertestamental Studies for CBQ is now a Jew, Professor Amy-Jill Levine of Vanderbilt!

It should be no surprise, then, that the major statement of the Pontifical Biblical Commission *The Jewish People and Their Sacred Scriptures in the Christian Bible* (2001)[7] argues persuasively that Jewish and Christian interpretations of Scripture, even where they appear to differ in their understanding of a given text of *Tanach*, can both be considered valid, in a parallel or analogical fashion. This, again, is a radical departure from past disputations. The Catholic Church, both through her theologians and through her official statements, has announced to all Catholics that they may and should learn important insights from Jewish tradition of biblical interpretation that they cannot learn from Christian tradition alone. The parallel for this on the Jewish side, of course, would be the remarkable statement, signed now by hundreds of Jewish scholars, *Dabru Emet*.[8]

Salvador, Brazil, June 7, 2004

18
Theological Dialogue
A Necessity, Not an Option

Pope John Paul II Cultural Center

The discussions we are concluding have touched on the deeper levels of our theological bridges that both unite and divide us as people of God. We are, we both believe, chosen by God to witness to, and to work to bring about, the ultimate end toward which all humanity and all creation groan, the *malchut shamayim*, the reign of God on earth. To make this witness to the world, we need to share with each other and in that sharing to deepen our understanding of the divine revelation that is our ancient heritage and living spiritual treasure. This revelation tells us of God and God's reaching out or covenanting with us, a covenanting that is the reason for and essence of our very being as communities of faith.

We share common Scriptures. Yet, much of what we share we see in light refracted differently through our intertwined yet divergent experiences of the one history of salvation of which we, the Church and the Jewish people, are but chapters. For it is God's history in the world, not our own, to which we witness.

We pray to the same God, or so we Christians affirm, the One God of Israel, the One God of Abraham and Sarah. And though we understand the Oneness of God differently, there are

117

linking points within the differences, points that our mystical and prayer traditions bridge but that our more prosaic, less analogically resonant theological language cannot always easily cross. We speak of "salvation" and "redemption." But do we reference the same realities, human and divine, in our speaking?

For centuries we have, each in our separateness from the other, thought we had within ourselves all the answers, and in the most profound sense we do. For we both have divine revelation and in that revelation, though we do not yet discern its fullness, lies the whole of Truth, a certain measure of the infinitude that our finite minds and words grasp, perhaps incompletely but for that no less certainly.

In dialogues such as the one just concluded, we learn that the one Infinite Truth we hold and cherish in order to pass on to future generations can be approached, described, and understood in more than one valid way. We learn how better to question and therefore to understand the revelation we cherish. Sometimes we learn more from the questions than from the answers. On the Christian side we ask, can it be coincidental to God's plan of salvation for humanity that the Jews survived throughout the centuries giving constant witness that there is One God and one destiny for humanity? Can it be coincidental that the Jews, more than decimated by the Shoah, emerged reborn to gather in their ancient Promised Land? Can it be coincidental that just before the destruction of Israel's sacred center, the Temple, an offshoot group of Jews espoused an impossible hope that God could become human to raise humanity from its own sins to new heights of holiness? Can Christianity be seen from a Jewish point of view as an aspect of Jewish history, a Jewish gift to humanity?

In this context of working together toward that deeper spiritual reconciliation that alone can provide the basis for trust and theological openness to each other's witness, the tragedies of our joint history and the times of mutual learning over the centuries need further study.

In *We Remember: A Reflection on the Shoah*, the Holy See stated, "The common future of Jews and Christians demands that we remember, for 'there is no future without memory.' History is itself *memoria futuri*."[1] This is to say that we remember the evils of the past not for the purpose of recrimination but for the sake of reconciliation. We remember and we repent not to be enmeshed in the guilt of previous generations, but to free future generations of Jews and Christians to go about the sacred work that God is calling us to do.

Washington, DC, March 15, 2005

Notes

(Note: The Appendix contains a list of the official Vatican or United States Bishops' documents cited in this book, along with the URLs at which the texts can be accessed. When references to these documents are given in the notes, the note directs the reader to the Appendix.)

1. MOBILIZATION FOR SOVIET JEWRY

1. Pope John Paul II, *Spiritual Pilgrimage: Texts on Jews and Judaism 1979–1995*, ed. Eugene J. Fisher and Leon Klenicki (New York: Crossroad, 1996), 109.

2. ANTI-DEFAMATION LEAGUE

1. Pope John Paul II, *On Jews and Judaism*, ed. Eugene Fisher and Leon Klenicki (Washington, DC: USCCB, 1982) was the first edition of this volume. The second edition was John Paul II, *Spiritual Pilgrimage: Texts on Jews and Judaism, 1979–1995*, ed. Eugene Fisher and Leon Klenicki (New York: Crossroad, 1996). The third and final edition of this volume, *The Saint for Shalom: How Pope John Paul II Transformed Catholic-Jewish Relations: His Complete Texts on Jews, Judaism and the State of Israel, 1975–2005*, ed. Eugene Fisher and Leon Klenicki (New

York: Crossroad/Anti-Defamation League, 2011), contains all of his statements, chronologically. See www.thesaintforshalom.com.

  2. See chapter 4, "Twenty-Five Years after *Nostra Aetate*," for a detailed description of this conciliar document.

  3. See chapter 9, "*We Remember*," for a more detailed account of the Waldheim affair.

3. INTRODUCTION OF ELIE WIESEL

  1. Editor's note: For the full text of Pope John Paul II's address to the Jews of Warsaw, see Pope John Paul II, *Spiritual Pilgrimage: Texts on Jews and Judaism, 1979–1995*, ed. Eugene J. Fisher and Leon Klenicki (New York: Crossroad, 1996), 98–99.

4. TWENTY-FIVE YEARS AFTER *NOSTRA AETATE*

  1. Excerpted from the *Proceedings of the Rabbinical Assembly* (New York: The Rabbinical Assembly, 1990), 87–106.

  2. Eugene Fisher, letter to Rabbi Mordecai Waxman, May 1990.

  3. Ibid.

5. UNION OF AMERICAN HEBREW CONGREGATIONS

  1. Now called the Union for Reform Judaism.

  2. Annette Daum and Eugene Fisher, *The Challenge of Shalom: A Dialogical Discussion Guide to the Catholic Bishops' Pastoral on Peace and War* (New York: Union of American Hebrew Congregations, and Washington, DC: The National Conference of Catholic Bishops, 1985).

  3. Editor's note: This was due to the reluctance on the part of Orthodox Judaism, then a part of the Synagogue Council of America, to participate in joint studies. The Orthodox groups have since left that organization. Its successor, the National Council of Synagogues, does

engage in theological dialogue with Christians, while the U.S. Catholic Bishops maintain an ongoing consultation with Orthodox Judaism centered on social issues.

4. The 1938 annual radio broadcast of the U.S. bishops; National Catholic News Service, November 17, 1938.

6. NATIONAL JEWISH COMMUNITY RELATIONS ADVISORY COUNCIL

1. See chapter 16, "Reflections on Anti-Semitism and the Church," for further details about Patriarch Michel Sabbah.

2. Accessible at http://www.lpj.org/newsite2006/patriarch/pastoral-letters/1990/prayforpeace.html.

7. ISRAEL BOND RALLY

1. *Crossing the Threshold of Hope* (New York: Alfred A. Knopf, 1994).

2. Fr. Henryk Jankowski (1936–2010), a Polish priest, achieved prominence in the 1980s by his support of Lech Walesa's Solidarity movement, but his reputation was later marred by a number of anti-Semitic comments that he made, one of which led to his being barred from preaching for a year.

3. Father Remi Hoeckman—of blessed memory [*editor*].

4. Pontifical Commission for Religious Relations with the Jews, "Guidelines and Suggestions for Implementing the Conciliar Declaration *Nostra Aetate*, no. 4," in Eugene J. Fisher, *Faith Without Prejudice: Rebuilding Christian Attitudes toward Judaism*, 2nd ed. (New York: Crossroad, 1993), 133–41. Also see by the Pontifical Commission for Religious Relations with the Jews, "Notes on the Correct Way to Present the Jews and Judaism in the Preaching and Catechesis of the Roman Catholic Church," in ibid., 144–57. See the Appendix for links to Web sites on which both these documents can be viewed online.

5. U.S. Conference of Catholic Bishops' Committee for Ecumenical and Interreligious Affairs, "Criteria for the Evaluation of Dramatizations of the Passion," in ibid., 185–94. See also U.S. Conference of Catholic Bishops' Committee on the Liturgy, "God's Mercy Endures Forever: Guidelines on the Presentation of Jews and Judaism in Catholic Preaching," in ibid., 170–85. See the Appendix for links to Web sites on which both these documents can be viewed online.

8. LESSONS TO LEARN FROM THE CATHOLIC RESCUERS

1. Editor's note: This was originally published in the documentary service of the Catholic News Service, *Origins* 26, no. 45 (May 1, 1997): 739–41.

2. See Ewa Kurek, *Your Life is Worth Mine: How Polish Nuns Saved Hundreds of Jewish Children in German-Occupied Poland, 1939–45* (New York: Hippocrene Books, 1997).

3. See Margherita Marchione, *Yours is a Precious Witness: Memoirs of Jews and Catholics in Wartime* (New York/Mahwah, NJ: Paulist Press, 1997).

4. Henri de Lubac (1896–1991), a Jesuit priest and a theologian, was appointed by Pope John XXIII as a consultant to the Preparatory Theological Commission for the Second Vatican Council and then served as a *peritus* (theological expert) to the Council itself. His writings in the field of ecclesiology were influential in the developing understanding of the Church as the entire people of God, not only the clergy. In 1983, Pope John Paul II named Father de Lubac a cardinal.

5. Carmelite Father Jacques de Jésus (1900–45), born Lucien Bunel, used his position as headmaster of the Petit Collège Sainte-Thérèse de l'Enfant-Jésus to help Jewish people during the Nazi occupation of France in the Second World War. Discovered by the Gestapo, he was arrested in 1944 and was imprisoned in several Nazi concentration camps. Though liberated by American troops in 1945, he died of tuberculosis a few weeks later, weighing only seventy-five pounds. Pere Jacques was named one of the "Righteous Among the Nations" in 1985.

9. *WE REMEMBER*

1. See the Appendix for the link to the online version of this document.

2. *Origins* 28, no. 2 (May 28, 1998): 28–32.

3. Cardinal Edward Idris Cassidy, "Reflections regarding the Vatican's Statement on the *Shoah*," in Secretariat for Ecumenical and Interreligious Affairs, *Catholics Remember the Holocaust* (Washington, DC: U.S. Catholic Conference, 1998), 65. Editor's note: This volume also contains the statements of various European bishops' conferences, as well as those issued in the United States, prior to the publication of *We Remember*. For the statement interpreting and implementing the Vatican document for the U.S. Church, see Secretariat for Ecumenical and Interreligious Affairs, *Catholic Teaching on the* Shoah (Washington, DC: U.S. Conference of Catholic Bishops, 2001). See the Appendix for links to Web sites on which these documents can be viewed online. The U.S. document carefully follows Cardinal Cassidy's interpretation of the Vatican document.

4. Cassidy, "Reflections regarding the Vatican's Statement on the *Shoah*," 64–65.

10. LOOKING TO THE FUTURE

1. Andrzej Micewski, *Cardinal Wyszynski: A Biography* (New York: Harcourt, Brace, Jovanovich, 1984), 34.

2. *Ecclesia in America* 50. Cf. Synod of Bishops, Special Assembly for Europe, Declaration *Ut Testes Sumus Christi Qui Nos Liberavit* (December 13, 1991), III; *S. Enchiridion Vaticanum*, 13, 635–55, *propositio* 62. See the Appendix for a link to a Web site for viewing the complete text of *Ecclesia in America* online.

3. Pope John Paul II's cover letter of March 12, 1998, on submitting the document *We Remember* to the Commission for Religious Relations with the Jews, in *Catholics Remember the Holocaust*, ed. Secretariat for Ecumenical and Interreligious Affairs, National Conference of Catholic

Bishops (Washington, DC: U.S. Catholic Conference Publication no. 5-290, 1998), 43.

    4. The 1938 annual radio broadcast of the U.S. bishops; National Catholic News Service, November 17, 1938.

    5. See chapter 11 in the present volume for Cardinal Cicognani's quote.

11. NATIONAL WORKSHOP ON CHRISTIAN-JEWISH RELATIONS

    1. Cited in J. Derek Homes, *The Papacy in the Modern World 1914–1978* (New York: Crossroad, 1981), 140.

    2. Gershon Greenberg, "American Catholics during the Holocaust," in *Peace/Shalom after Atrocity: Proceedings of the First Scholars' Conference on the Teaching of the Holocaust* (Greensburg, PA: Seton Hill College, the National Catholic Center for Holocaust Education, April 1989), 37–51.

12. NATIONAL JEWISH COUNCIL FOR PUBLIC AFFAIRS

    1. John Tracy Ellis, *The Life of James Cardinal Gibbons: Archbishop of Baltimore, 1834–1921*, vol. 1 (Milwaukee, WI: Bruce Publishing Company, 1952), 309.

13. JAY PHILLIPS CENTER FOR JEWISH-CHRISTIAN LEARNING

    1. *John Paul II in the Holy Land: In His Own Words*, Lawrence Boadt, CSP, and Kevin di Camillo, eds. (Mahwah, NJ: Paulist Press, 2005), 104–5, 106.

14. COVENANT AND MISSION

1. See chapter 4, "Twenty-Five Years after *Nostra Aetate*," for details about this document of the Second Vatican Council.

2. Cf. Gian Franco Svidercosch, *Letter to a Jewish Friend: The Simple and Extraordinary Story of Pope John Paul II and His Jewish School Friend* (New York: Crossroad, 1995).

3. Ibid., 88.

4. Pontifical Commission for Religious Relations with the Jewish People, "Guidelines and Suggestions for Implementing the Conciliar Declaration *Nostra Aetate*, no. 4," 1974.

5. Pope John Paul II, *Spiritual Pilgrimage: Texts on Jews and Judaism 1979–1995*, ed. Eugene J. Fisher and Leon Klenicki (New York: Crossroad, 1996), 5.

6. In *Fifteen Years of Catholic-Jewish Dialogue, 1970–1985: Selected Papers*, International Catholic-Jewish Liaison Committee (Vatican City State: Libreria Editrice Vatican and Libreria Editrice Lateranense, 1988), 46–62; quotation at 52–54.

7. Available at: http://www.bc.edu/dam/files/research_sites/cjl/texts/cjrelations/resources/documents/interreligious/ncs_usccb120802.htm.

8. All of the following quotations until the end of the chapter are from Cardinal Kasper from his address titled "The Commission for Religious Relations with the Jews: A Crucial Endeavour of the Catholic Church," given November 6, 2002, at Boston College. For the entire address, see http://www.vatican.va/roman_curia/pontifical_councils/chrstuni/card-kasper-docs/rc_pc_chrstuni_doc_20021106_kasper-boston-college_en.html.

9. See Appendix for the Web site address for this document.

16. REFLECTIONS ON ANTI-SEMITISM AND THE CHURCH

1. The full text of this article can be found at: http://www.bc.edu/dam/files/research_sites/cjl/texts/cjrelations/resources/articles/Keeler_antisem_June04.htm.

2. "Declaration on the Relationship of the Church to Non-Christian Religions," *Nostra Aetate,* no. 4 (October 28, 1965). See Appendix. The use here of the word *fraternal,* or "brotherly," is intentionally theological to show the intimacy of the Church's relationship with the Jewish people.

3. "Guidelines and Suggestions for Implementing the Conciliar Declaration *Nostra Aetate,* no. 4" (December 1, 1974); "Notes on the Correct Way to Present the Jews and Judaism in the Preaching and Catechesis of the Roman Catholic Church" (June 24, 1985); *We Remember: A Reflection on the Shoah* (March 16, 1998). See the Appendix to access online versions of all of these documents. Cf. International Catholic-Jewish Liaison Committee, *Fifteen Years of Catholic-Jewish Dialogue, 1970–1985* (Vatican City: Libreria Editrice Vaticana & Libreria Editrice Lateranense, 1988). Such dialogues provided the basis for the statements' understanding of Jews and Judaism.

4. For example, the Delegates of Episcopal Conferences and Other Experts in Catholic-Jewish Relations (March 6, 1982).

5. "Notes on the Correct Way to Present the Jews and Judaism in the Preaching and Catechesis of the Roman Catholic Church" (June 24, 1985), no. 25. See the Appendix.

6. Pope John Paul II at the Great Synagogue of Rome, April 13, 1986.

7. The statements of European and U.S. bishops can be found in Secretariat for Ecumenical and Interreligious Affairs, *Catholics Remember the Holocaust* (Washington, DC: U.S. Catholic Conference, 1998).

8. John Paul II to Jewish leaders, Miami, September 11, 1986.

9. Pope John Paul II cited in *We Remember*, III, 6.

10. See www.bc.edu/research/cjl.

11. See Jules Isaac, *Jesus and Israel* (New York: Holt, Rinehart and Winston, 1971).

12. See the Appendix.

13. *We Remember*, III, 6.

14. Address to the Vatican Symposium on the "Roots of Anti-Judaism in the Christian Milieu," October 13, 1997.

15. Genesis 1:27.

16. Galatians 3:28–29. The exception of the Spanish *limpia de raza* (purity of blood), with its tragic consequences, deserves special study.

17. In Eva Fleischner, ed., *Auschwitz: Beginning of a New Era?* (New York: KTAV, 1973), 105.

18. *Nostra Aetate*, no. 4.

19. John Paul II, "Address to the New Ambassador of the Federal Republic of Germany to the Holy See," November 1980.

20. Yad Vashem in Israel and the U.S. Holocaust Memorial Museum in Washington preserve the memory of many more of these "righteous Gentiles."

21. "The Church and Racism," no. 15. Text and commentary can be found in Eugene Fisher and Leon Klenicki, *Antisemitism is a Sin* (New York: Anti-Defamation League, 1990). See the Appendix for a link to read the document online.

22. Drew Christiansen, "A Campaign to Divide the Church in the Holy Land," *America*, May 19, 2003. Available at http://www.america magazine.org/content/article.cfm?article_id=2976.

23. Accessible at http://www.bc.edu/dam/files/research_sites/cjl/ texts/cjrelations/resources/articles/Kasper_Sep_03.htm.

24. *Ecclesia in Europa* (June 28, 2003), no. 56. See the Appendix for the Web site for the full text.

17. A DEVELOPING AGENDA

1. The full text of this paper can be found at: http://www.bc.edu/ dam/files/research_sites/cjl/texts/cjrelations/resources/articles/Keeler_ agenda_June04.htm.

2. Scharper, *Torah and Gospel*, 27. Both Baum and Sheering over the years modified their views to accept a greater amount of continuity between Christian anti-Judaism and Nazi anti-Semitism.

3. See the Appendix for the link to the online version.

4. Available at http://www.bc.edu/dam/files/research_sites/cjl/ texts/cjrelations/resources/documents/catholic/church_Racism.html.

5. See Eugene Fisher, ed., *The Jewish Roots of Christian Liturgy* (Mahwah, NJ: Paulist Press, 1983).

6. For example, Joseph Gutmann, "Christian Influences on Jewish Customs," in Leon Klenicki and Gabe Huck, eds., *Spirituality and Prayer: Jewish and Christian Understandings* (Mahwah, NJ: Paulist Press, 1983), 128–38.

7. See Appendix.

8. The text of and the commentaries on *Dabru Emet* can be found on the Web site http://www.bc.edu/content/bc/research/cjl/cjrelations/back groundresources/documents/jewish.html.

18. THEOLOGICAL DIALOGUE

1. See Appendix.

Appendix
Document Web Sites

Following is a list of the official Vatican or United States Bishops' documents cited in this book, along with the URLs at which the texts can be accessed.

Catholic Teaching on the Shoah: Implementing the Holy See's We Remember. February 2001. http://old.usccb.org/seia/we_remember.pdf.

"The Church and Racism: Towards a More Fraternal Society." February 1989. A summary of the document is at http://www.bc.edu/dam/files/research_sites/cjl/texts/cjrelations/resources/documents/catholic/church_Racism.html. The full 1988 document can be accessed at http://www.ewtn.com/library/curia/pcjpraci.htm. Over a decade later (2001), the Vatican added a new introduction to the document, which can be accessed at http://www.vatican.va/roman_curia/pontifical_councils/justpeace/documents/rc_pc_justpeace_doc_20010829_comunicato-razzismo_en.html.

"The Commission for Religious Relations with the Jews: A Crucial Endeavour of the Catholic Church." Reflections by Cardinal Walter Kasper. November 6, 2002. http://www.vatican.va/roman_curia/pontifical_councils/chrstuni/card-kasper-docs/rc_pc_chrstuni_doc_20021106_kasper-boston-college_en.html.

"Criteria for the Evaluation of Dramatizations of the Passion." 1988, accessible at http://www.bc.edu/content/dam/files/research_sites/cjl/texts/cjrelations/resources/documents/catholic/Passion_Plays.htm.

Ecclesia in America. January 22, 1999. http://www.vatican.va/holy_father/ john_paul_ii/apost_exhortations/documents/hf_jp-ii_exh_ 22011999_ecclesia-in-america_en.html.

Ecclesia in Europa. June 28, 2003. http://www.vatican.va/holy_father/ john_paul_ii/apost_exhortations/documents/hf_jp-ii_exh_ 20030628_ecclesia-in-europa_en.html.

"God's Mercy Endures Forever: Guidelines on the Presentation of Jews and Judaism in Catholic Preaching." 1988. http://old.usccb.org/ liturgy/godsmercy.shtml.

"Guidelines and Suggestions for Implementing the Conciliar Declaration *Nostra Aetate,* no. 4," December 1, 1974. http://www. vatican.va/roman_curia/pontifical_councils/chrstuni/relations-jews-docs/rc_pc_chrstuni_doc_19741201_nostra-aetate_en.html.

The Jewish People and Their Sacred Scriptures in the Christian Bible. http://www.vatican.va/roman_curia/congregations/cfaith/pcb_do cuments/rc_con_cfaith_doc_20020212_popolo-ebraico_en.html.

Nostra Aetate (Declaration on the Relation of the Church to Non-Christian Religions), October 28, 1965. http://www.vatican.va/ archive/hist_councils/ii_vatican_council/documents/vat-ii_decl_ 19651028_nostra-aetate_en.html.

"Notes on the Correct Way to Present the Jews and Judaism in the Preaching and Catechesis of the Roman Catholic Church." June 24, 1985. http://www.vatican.va/roman_curia/pontifical_councils/ chrstuni/relations-jews-docs/rc_pc_chrstuni_doc_19820306_jews-judaism_en.html.

We Remember: A Reflection on the Shoah. March 16, 1998. http://www. vatican.va/roman_curia/pontifical_councils/chrstuni/documents/rc_ pc_chrstuni_doc_16031998_shoah_en.html.

Clemens Thoma and Michael Wyschogrod, editors, *Parable and Story in Judaism and Christianity* (A Stimulus Book, 1989).

Eugene J. Fisher and Leon Klenicki, editors, *In Our Time: The Flowering of Jewish-Catholic Dialogue* (A Stimulus Book, 1990).

David Burrell and Yehezkel Landau, editors, *Voices from Jerusalem* (A Stimulus Book, 1991).

Leon Klenicki, editor, *Toward A Theological Encounter* (A Stimulus Book, 1991).

John Rousmaniere, *A Bridge to Dialogue: The Story of Jewish-Christian Relations*, edited by James A. Carpenter and Leon Klenicki (A Stimulus Book, 1991).

Michael E. Lodahl, *Shekhinah/Spirit* (A Stimulus Book, 1992).

George M. Smiga, *Pain and Polemic: Anti-Judaism in the Gospels* (A Stimulus Book, 1992).

Eugene J. Fisher, editor, *Interwoven Destinies: Jews and Christians Through the Ages* (A Stimulus Book, 1993).

Anthony Kenny, *Catholics, Jews and the State of Israel* (A Stimulus Book, 1993).

Bernard J. Lee, SM, *Jesus and the Metaphors of God: The Christs of the New Testament*, Conversation on the Road Not Taken, Vol. 2 (A Stimulus Book, 1993).

Eugene J. Fisher, editor, *Visions of the Other: Jewish and Christian Theologians Assess the Dialogue* (A Stimulus Book, 1995).

Leon Klenicki and Geoffrey Wigoder, editors, *A Dictionary of the Jewish-Christian Dialogue*, Expanded Edition (A Stimulus Book, 1995).

Vincent Martin, *A House Divided: The Parting of the Ways between Synagogue and Church* (A Stimulus Book, 1995).

Philip A. Cunningham and Arthur F. Starr, editors, *Sharing Shalom: A Process for Local Interfaith Dialogue Between Christians and Jews* (A Stimulus Book, 1998).

Frank E. Eakin, Jr., *What Price Prejudice? Christian Antisemitism in America* (A Stimulus Book, 1998).

Ekkehard Schuster and Reinhold Boschert-Kimmig, *Hope Against Hope: Johann Baptist Metz and Elie Wiesel Speak Out on the Holocaust* (A Stimulus Book, 1999).

Mary C. Boys, *Has God Only One Blessing? Judaism as a Source of Christian Understanding* (A Stimulus Book, 2000).

Avery Dulles, SJ, and Leon Klenicki, editors, *The Holocaust, Never to Be Forgotten: Reflections on the Holy See's Document* We Remember (A Stimulus Book, 2000).

Johannes Reuchlin, *Recommendation Whether to Confiscate, Destroy and Burn All Jewish Books: A Classic Treatise against Anti-Semitism*, translated, edited, and with an introduction by Peter Wortsman (A Stimulus Book, 2000).

Philip A. Cunningham, *A Story of Shalom: The Calling of Christians and Jews by a Covenanting God* (A Stimulus Book, 2001).

Philip A. Cunningham, *Sharing the Scriptures*, The Word Set Free, Vol. 1 (A Stimulus Book, 2003).

Dina Wardi, *Auschwitz: Contemporary Jewish and Christian Encounters* (A Stimulus Book, 2003).

Michael Lotker, *A Christian's Guide to Judaism* (A Stimulus Book, 2004).

Lawrence Boadt and Kevin di Camillo, editors, *John Paul II in the Holy Land: In His Own Words: With Christian and Jewish Perspectives by Yehezkel Landau and Michael McGarry, CSP* (A Stimulus Book, 2005).

James K. Aitken and Edward Kessler, editors, *Challenges in Jewish-Christian Relations* (A Stimulus Book, 2006).

George M. Smiga, *The Gospel of John Set Free: Preaching without Anti-Judaism* (A Stimulus Book, 2008).

Daniel J. Harrington, SJ, *The Synoptic Gospels Set Free: Preaching without Anti-Judaism* (A Stimulus Book, 2009).

Richard C. Lux, *The Jewish People, the Holy Land, and the State of Israel: A Catholic View* (A Stimulus Book, 2009).

Jean Duchesne, editor, *Cardinal Jean-Marie Lustiger on Christians and Jews* (A Stimulus Book, 2010).

Pope Benedict XVI, *Pope Benedict XVI, Pope Benedict XVI in the Holy Land* (A Stimulus Book, 2011).

Franklin Sherman, editor, *Bridges: Documents on the Christian-Jewish Dialogue* (A Stimulus Book, 2011).

STIMULUS BOOKS are developed by the Stimulus Foundation, a not-for-profit organization, and are published by Paulist Press. The Foundation wishes to further the publication of scholarly books on Jewish and Christian topics that are of importance to Judaism and Christianity.

The Stimulus Foundation was established by an erstwhile refugee from Nazi Germany who intends to contribute with these publications to the improvement of communication between Jews and Christians.

Books for publication in this Series will be selected by a committee of the Foundation, and offers of manuscripts and works in progress should be addressed to:

The Stimulus Foundation
c/o Paulist Press
997 Macarthur Boulevard
Mahwah, N.J. 07430
www.paulistpress.com